7 Steps

2nd Edition

to a Language-Rich, Interactive Classroom

John Seidlitz & Bill Perryman
With contributions from
Sharon R. Goldman, EdD

Published by Seidlitz Education
P.O. Box 166827
Irving, TX 75016
www.seidlitzeducation.com

For related titles and support materials visit www.seidlitzeducation.com.

5.23

ACKNOWLEDGEMENTS

First and foremost, it is important to express our thanks to the many skilled educators and leaders in districts throughout the United States and across the globe who have shared their classrooms, ideas, and suggestions with us over the past ten years since the first edition was published. We are grateful for the ongoing opportunities to help educators create classrooms where all their students can grow in the acquisition of academic language.

We owe a great deal of gratitude to all those who work with Seidlitz Education: Meg White and Sarah Welch, who helped ensure this book was well crafted; Anna Matis who developed the new teacher-friendly features; Anne-Charlotte Patterson, who fashioned them into the book's graphics and design; Sharon Goldman, who designed and implemented the research study that informed many of the changes found in this edition; Mónica Lara and Nancy Motley, who provided feedback and suggestions that have influenced our thinking on both the implementation and the meaning of the core ideas found in this book. We also want to specifically thank all the educators and leaders whose contributions appear in this book, including Marcy Voss for her additions addressing higher-order thinking skills, Stephen Fleenor for his work on the Coaching appendix, and Allison Hand for her revision of the content and language objectives section, as well as the rest of the team at Seidlitz Education for their tireless work helping teachers bring these strategies to life in their classrooms.

In addition, we want to thank and acknowledge ELLevation Education, Northside ISD, and East Central ISD, who provided the videos of teachers implementing the steps in classrooms.

We will always be grateful for the support and learning opportunities provided by leaders whose work focuses on ways to improve instruction for language learners, including Deborah Short, Jana Echevarria, Mary Ellen Vogt, and many others. We have learned (and continue to learn) so much from educators and leaders in this field.

"7 Steps has changed the way we design instruction in Alvin ISD. ALL kids are academic language learners, and we have used 7 Steps to make content comprehensible while building academic language for ALL kids. Every teacher at every level uses 7 Steps - it is the expectation."

Ashley Gomez
District EL Specialist
Alvin ISD

Table of Contents

PREFACE by John Seidlitz

It's been an incredible 10 years since the first *7 Steps to a Language-Rich, Interactive Classroom* was published. The core ideas found in the book originally flowed from a fusion of my work with teachers of English learners and Bill Perryman's work with content-area teachers. We were committed to helping teachers implement effective strategies grounded in research to help all students develop academic language. We had both observed that creating a language-rich, interactive classroom was in some ways easier and in other ways more challenging than teachers often understood. Educators easily grasped the need for strategies that helped all students develop academic language; what they found challenging was learning how to get started and how to make those practices a reality in their classrooms.

For two years we collaborated with teachers to identify which research-based practices could be easily implemented to maximize language development. The core practices we identified became the *7 Steps to a Language-Rich, Interactive Classroom*. We sincerely hoped that the book would help to bridge the gap between what research shows is effective and what we saw happening in schools. We continue to be amazed by the results we've seen. I am astonished that, just a decade later, the book has sold over 100,000 copies and that the central practices of the 7 Steps are being implemented in over 1,000 school districts across the United States and in countries around the world.

Districts had long shared anecdotal data on how the method was helping not only multilingual learners but also students with learning disabilities and economically disadvantaged students to improve performance on required state assessments.

We had also heard reports about how English learners in Texas were advancing more quickly in language proficiency when teachers were using the 7 Steps. Two years ago we decided to launch a multi-year, multi-district research study to see how effective the method really was. We have been amazed by the first phase of the results. English learners who were students of teachers trained and coached in implementing the 7 Steps significantly outperformed students of teachers who were not similarly trained and coached. This held true for math tests, reading tests, and assessments of English language acquisition. The results, which were presented at the 2021 annual meeting of the American Education Research Association, are outlined in the appendix in Part 2 of this book.

Part of the motivation for publishing this 10th anniversary edition was to share this research, as well as all that we've learned from so many leaders in education over the past 10 years. In addition to some updated research and ideas in the text, the book also includes the following:

» Guidance for integrating strategies into virtual classrooms

» Videos from classrooms across the country using the 7 Steps in instruction, including those generously shared by ELLevation Education

» Testimonials from teachers and school leaders in the field who offer their insight on the effectiveness and positive impact of using the 7 Steps in their classrooms, schools, and districts

» The use of the term "multilingual learners," except in cases referencing research that was conducted specific to English learners

» Specific methods for facilitating higher-order thinking through the 7 Steps •

Introduction by Bill Perryman

Sixth grade was not my favorite year in elementary school. When I entered my homeroom class on the first day of the school year, I noticed mountains of worksheets stacked at the back of the room. They were an omen for what was to come.

In sixth grade, we changed classes for our core subjects every day, but each classroom looked the same, with students' desks in rows and the teacher's desk at the front of the room. Interaction among students was nonexistent, except when we finished our assignments and had a chance to visit with one another. Class dynamics and participation were similar with every instructor. The teacher would call on one student at a time while the rest of us zoned out, patiently waiting for that one lone response.

In science class, we took notes all year long but did few, if any, experiments. In English class, we labored through a boring and complicated workbook until I almost felt illiterate! And math was a complete disaster. One month, the teacher stopped teaching math to have us research famous mathematicians. This exercise turned into…you guessed it: a written report. Social studies class was no better. Remember that mountain of worksheets at the back of the room? We climbed that mountain for one whole year.

But things were about to change. Fast-forward a few years to my high school biology teacher. She was a great teacher, passionate about science and teaching. She provided an interactive, "hands-on" classroom with engaging and fun lessons. In her classroom, we worked in groups to complete actual experiments. She helped us learn science in a way that made sense. In fact, her lessons will be with me for the rest of my life. With my biology teacher, I experienced the best of teaching: engagement; higher-level thinking; a warm, safe environment; and passionate delivery of the content.

As a teenager, I liked my biology class because it was engaging and fun. As I studied educational methods over the years, I came to understand why my biology teacher was so successful. The way she taught matched the way our brains learn. Many years later, her teaching methods would come to be supported by scientific research. The impact of this research has been groundbreaking, and its implications for education remain invaluable. For teachers, it means that we can tailor education to meet student needs. This sounds like a simple concept, but it has been a long time in the making.

We have known for a long time that students need to stand, move, and share their knowledge with one another. We need to provide adequate time for reflection. We need to add novelty and excitement to our lessons. We need to teach students the learning strategies that will help them find success in the real world. But are we hearing the message? A classic study of 1,500 American classrooms (Schmoker, 2006) produced startling data. It showed that in 85 percent of the classrooms, less than half of the students were paying attention. Only 3 percent of the classrooms showed evidence of higher-level thinking activities, and over half of the lessons focused primarily on worksheets.

The leading problem with worksheet "drill and kill" education is its negative effect on students–especially our most marginalized students. These exercises convince kids that school is not a place where they want to be. Instead of drill and kill exercises, instruction needs to be creative and filled with positive emotion, and it needs to challenge young minds. "A recent study...in England found that the ability to read well is the single best indicator of future economic success–regardless of family background" (Schmoker, 2006, p. 57). When students become literate and articulate, they will enjoy learning, and they will succeed.

Literacy is paramount in the quest for an educated citizenry in a democratic society. It is the ticket to success and the ability to advocate for oneself and advance. When we prepare students to speak and write coherently, we are preparing them to be successful in life. As a teacher and an educational consultant, I have begun to see the importance of argumentative literacy.

Argumentative literacy could be described as an individual's ability to engage in a coherent discussion, to articulate ideas, and to defend or support an idea or issue

intelligently with breadth and depth. This includes the ability to step inside someone else's shoes and to see things from their perspective, a trait that is foreign to many of us (Wiggins & McTighe, 1998). It is the exact opposite of narrow-minded partisanship.

Literacy instruction, however, is more than just having students read words on a page. It also includes the ability to engage students in meaningful conversations and to have them write with power and purpose in authentic situations. Educational researchers are increasingly paying attention to the significance of classroom discussion and its relationship to literacy (Graff, 2008; Rose, 1989). While I have always worked to foster a learning atmosphere in which students are actively engaged, focusing on argumentative literacy adds another dimension of purpose and mission to my teaching.

When I began working with John Seidlitz, I quickly learned that we shared a passion for the art of teaching. John was as passionate about academic literacy, especially for English learners, as I was about meaningful student interaction for all students. We began to collaborate, and we discovered ways to combine a focus on student interaction with academic literacy. What we created was a seven-step procedure that all teachers can use to create interactive, language-rich, and highly engaging classrooms. The 7 steps outlined in the following chapters provide examples of these important concepts. •

Part 1:
The 7 Steps

1 Teach students what to say when they
  don't know what to say.

2 Have students speak in complete sentences.

3 Randomize and rotate when calling on students.

4 Use total response signals to check for understanding.

5 Use visuals and vocabulary strategies that
  support your objectives.

6 Have students participate in structured conversations.

7 Have students participate in structured
  reading and writing activities.

Step 1

Teach students what to say when they don't know what to say.

As teachers who work with students from diverse backgrounds, one of the biggest challenges facing us is the phenomenon known as learned helplessness. Students sometimes feel overwhelmed with a sense of powerlessness about their negative situation and stop attempting to turn the situation around and succeed. In fact, it is all too common that we as teachers inadvertently train students to not even try. Every time we ask students to respond to a question or perform a task, and fail to hold them accountable for their responses or actions, we send them a message: you are not expected to try, much less do well.

CONSIDER THE FOLLOWING SCENARIO
Imagine for a moment that a principal asks a group of third-grade teachers to gather specific data on students from various subpopulations. The teachers look at the request and realize they don't know how to find information on the students. As a result, they write on the form, "We don't know," and put it in the principal's box.

How do you think the principal would react? In the professional world, such behavior would never be acceptable. As teachers, we have all been frustrated when students are called on, and they either maintain a long silence as they stare at the floor, shrug their shoulders, or say,

"I don't know." Rather than simply accepting the non-answer of "I don't know," we can instill in our students a sense of accountability and teach them how to help themselves. By encouraging students and providing support for them to simply attempt a response or action, we enable them to overcome learned helplessness and really become independent learners.

However, it is not enough to just tell students to think for themselves and try harder. We need to guide our students through the language and habits of independent learners so they, too, can become independent learners. Teaching our students how to acquire helpful information when they are confused -- and teaching them to think about the steps involved in reaching a specific goal -- gives them skills they can use inside and outside of school.

We are all looking for ways to banish "I don't know," "Huh?," and "What?" from our classrooms. One simple solution is to teach students how to respond when they are unsure about an answer for a question without using "I don't know." There are a number of specific alternatives that can help students get past the "I don't know" stage. Providing these alternatives, teaching students how to use them, and holding them accountable for using them creates an expectation of accountable conversation.

HERE'S HOW IT WORKS

Provide students with these alternative responses to saying "I Don't Know," and create a classroom routine around their use.

What to Say Instead of "I Don't Know."

> May I please have some more information?

> May I please have some time to think?

> Would you please repeat the question?

> Where could I find more information about that?

> May I ask a friend for help?

On the first or second day of school, demonstrate how to use the responses and explain the routine. The goal here is to emphasize that all students are responsible for participating. You might consider creating a poster that includes all of the responses.

After modeling how to use the responses, explain what is meant by the expectation of accountable conversation. Whenever a teacher asks a question, students have two choices: either respond to the teacher with an answer or request assistance and then respond. The important principle is that students must always respond. They might not respond correctly, and they might need some extra time or support, but opting out of the conversation is not an option.

What to say instead of "IDK"

? May I please have some more information?

? May I please have some time to think?

? Would you please repeat the question?

? Where could I find some more information about that?

? May I please ask a friend for help?

WHAT RESEARCH SAYS

Teaching students what to say when they don't know what to say is a metacognitive strategy. Research shows that when learners use metacognitive strategies in the classroom to regulate the process of their knowledge acquisition, academic performance is positively impacted (Boekaerts et al., 2000; Haukås et al., 2018). Developing metacognitive skills where students can monitor their own thinking and understanding purposefully and then choose how to access help requires thoughtful planning (Perry et al., 2019; Snow et al., 2005; Vogt & Nagano, 2003). Essentially, building internal monitoring systems by offering students alternatives regarding what to say instead of "I don't know," then modeling the use of various responses to demonstrate when and why students should use the responses supports metacognitive development.

This is particularly important for students learning English as a second language (Chamot, 2005; Haukås et al., 2018). Teaching English learners to take conscious steps to understand what they are doing in the process of learning will result in far greater success in content language development and acquisition (Echavarría et al., 2017; Zhang & Zhang, 2018). To support ELs in building English language skills, teachers must actively engage students in developing metacognitive strategies by modeling and explaining how to use them effectively (Calderón et al., 2011; Lipson & Wixson, 2008).

Step it UP!

After initially introducing the expectation of accountable conversations to students and using the poster of alternative responses in the classroom, we're ready to STEP IT UP. It's time to branch out and teach students what to say when they don't know what to say in other ways beyond what's listed on the poster. The basic idea is to prompt students to create their own sentences and questions to use in different situations so that they can independently seek help when needed. We can simply provide time to ask students what questions they might have before, during, or after an activity. For example, we might ask, "What can you do if you're confused during this activity?" or "What will you do if you don't understand someone in your discussion group?" The chart below provides more examples of this:

	Questions students might ask	Purpose
Science	What is my job during this step?	Help and clarification during a lab
Language Arts	Could you please try to explain that in a different way?	Ask another student for clarification while in small group settings
Kindergarten homeroom	Can you show me how to __?	Help in the lunchroom, on the playground, or on the way to the bus

We can also encourage our students to get in the habit of telling us what they already do know when they ask us for more information. Students can evaluate their own understanding and then take ownership by targeting the parts of a question they are (or may not be) able to answer. They may respond by saying things like this:

"Well, I started working out the problem by _____, but I was unsure what to do next."

"I think that _____ is the answer because _____."

"I know _____, but I'm trying to figure out _____."

Building confidence in students requires them to believe we will honor their responses for what they do know. By praising anything of value that they add to the lesson, we can engage students in rich, content-appropriate responses. Guiding them to richer responses will help them go just a little bit further when sharing their own background knowledge and experiences.

Frequently Asked Questions

(1) **How can we help students move toward evaluating what they "don't know" and creating their own questions?**

Once the "What to Say Instead of I Don't Know" support system is in place, we can start prompting students to get in the habit of evaluating their own level of understanding and creating their own questions. Having students create their own questions can be an effective way to build student capacity to develop their own internal dialogue (Crowell & Kuhn, 2014; Chohan, 2010). It can be helpful to provide examples and models of what it looks like to generate questions in an academic context. Using the "think aloud" strategy is a great way to demonstrate how learners create questions. Here's how it might look:

WATCH
The Power of Step 1 at
Legacy Middle School

Eighth Grade Social Studies Dialogue
STUDENTS CREATING QUESTIONS

TEACHER Let's read these quotes from Sojourner Truth together:
"Truth is powerful, and it prevails."
"If women want any rights more than they've got, why don't they just take them, and not be talking about it?"
"I am not going to die, I'm going home like a shooting star."
"It is the mind that makes the body."

TEACHER (*Continues*) I understand she's concerned about women's rights, but I'm also wondering about some other questions I have about these quotes.

(*Teacher "thinks aloud" her questions.*)
What is it that I don't understand? Hmm...I'm also wondering why she brought up the word "truth"? Was something dishonest happening?
Show me thumbs up when you are ready to tell me something you are wondering about these quotes.
(*Teacher randomly selects Leo.*)

LEO I'm wondering what rights she's talking about. Could women vote back then?

TEACHER Good question, Leo. How could we find out?

LEO We need to look up when she gave this speech and then when women got the right to vote in the United States.

TEACHER Why don't you check real quick and then get back to us? In the meantime, who would you like to hear from?

LEO I'd like to hear from...Alex.

TEACHER Alex, can you share your thoughts with us? What are you wondering about?

ALEX I want to know if she was about to die or something. Was she really old when she said this?

Engagement at this higher level of responding will indeed cause students to learn how to "think on their feet," and engagement levels will soar as they realize there are so many ways to deepen their thinking processes. Setting up a system of support that encourages engagement–not just attention–teaches students the language and habits of thinkers!

 2 **How much information should I give when students ask for help?**

The goal is for students to participate as independent learners, so it's important to give only what is required to accomplish that goal. We want to support students, not enable them. Scaffolding is the support that leads to independence. Enabling is the support that leads to dependence. The most important thing to keep in mind is that scaffolding is temporary. Pauline Gibbons asks us to imagine that linguistic scaffolding is much like the support that is "essential for the successful construction of the building" (Gibbons, 2015).

Sometimes specific situations dictate when we might need to give most (or all) of the information to a student to get a response. These include absence the day before, lack of understanding of concepts or language, or a severe learning disability.

For other learning situations, our focus is to give students the tools to answer questions without help. We might tell a student, "Look in your notes, and I'll get back to you in a minute," or "Let me give you a minute to think, and I'll get back to you." Sometimes when students ask for help, we can simply reword or rephrase the question in simpler terms so they will be able to respond.

Take a look at this sample teacher-student dialogue with a high level of scaffolding for a beginning English learner in a sheltered math class:

Sixth Grade Math Dialogue
SUPPORTING STUDENTS WHO "DON'T KNOW"

TEACHER Lucas, what is the first step we might take in solving this equation?

LUCAS I don't know. *(Teacher points to the poster with alternate responses.)* Oh...Can I please have some more information?

TEACHER Sure. Everyone, look at your notes from yesterday. See if you can figure out the first step we would take to solve this equation. *(Teacher walks over to Lucas's desk while students are looking in their notebooks. She points to the parentheses in the equation and speaks softly to Lucas.)* The first step is to simplify each side by removing the parentheses. Can you repeat that for me?

LUCAS *(Pointing to the parentheses.)* Yeah...The first step is to simplify by removing the parentheses.

TEACHER Good. Okay, class, let me get your attention. *(Speaking in front of the whole class.)* Lucas, can you tell me the first step in solving this equation?

LUCAS The first step is to simplify by removing the parentheses.

TEACHER Thanks. Can someone show us what that looks like?

Will this strategy become a crutch for students who overuse it?

It could if we don't remain focused on independent learning as the goal. Gradually withdrawing the support we provide when students use the strategy is key. However, we want to be careful about being too quick to judge students' motives, because they may need more assistance than we think. When it appears that a student is always asking for help before responding independently, we can say, "I think you can find out on your own. Look in your notes, and I'll call on you when you show me a thumbs-up."

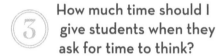

How much time should I give students when they ask for time to think?

It's easiest to have students let us know (after asking for time to think) when they have had enough time. This can be accomplished by asking for a specific signal to show they are ready; for example, the teacher could say, "Sure, you can have more time. Just show me a thumbs-up as soon as you're ready," or "Sure. Take some time, and just close your book when you're ready to respond." After students have asked for time, always be sure they are ready before calling on them again, eliminating the potential for embarrassing a student who isn't ready. If a particular student still needs help after a few minutes, walk over to their desk and provide one-on-one support. Another alternative is to allow students to talk to each other in a Turn & Tell Five (see p. 20) exercise so that the student who needs more time can get input from his peers before responding.

WATCH
Turn & Tell Five
in Ms. Kayem's
Classroom

What do you do with students who absolutely refuse to respond?

It is important to pinpoint why the students are not willing to respond. Sometimes we may think students are noncompliant when they simply don't understand what we ask them to do or they didn't hear the question. Early on, some students may be embarrassed to use a new strategy for fear of looking awkward in front of their peers. When they realize that everyone is required to use this strategy in class, it becomes easier for them to participate. If we have students who are shy or are multilingual learners, we can have them repeat after us or speak softly at first so that only we, the teachers, can hear them. We also need to consider that some students acquiring a new language may be in their silent period and may need time to adjust to the sounds and rhythms of the new language. The easiest way to get our noncompliant students to use alternatives to saying "I don't know" is to act as if they plan to participate. Just smile politely and respectfully, and ask them, "Please use one of these strategies." Then wait. If they flatly refuse, model the strategy and ask again, letting tone and body language communicate the expectation that they will participate. If this doesn't work, it's time to look at other options:

» Holding a private conference with the student

» Finding out if there are other issues at play

» Moving ahead with another classroom management system already in place

Keep in mind any special circumstances or considerations for students with special needs, which could preclude participation in this strategy.

 What about students with special needs? Do they have to respond as well?

As a general rule, we have found that all students can follow the accountability rule. If a student's individualized education plan or disability makes it impossible for her to participate, adjustments are needed. We want to be very careful here. Many times, students are capable of more than we imagine when given a chance.

 Won't some students always ask a friend for help and then become too dependent on others?

It depends on the student and the situation. Sometimes when you are working with multilingual learners, students who are reticent to speak in front of others, or students with special needs, it can be beneficial to allow particular students to depend on peers for extended support while learning a new language and subject matter. If students consistently ask, "May I ask a friend for help?" and we believe they can be more independent, we say, "I think you know this. Why don't you think about it for just a minute, and I'll get back to you." If we see that support is still needed, we can walk to the desk and provide one-on-one support, or we can direct the student to resources that can provide information.

Will these strategies slow down my instruction as I assist struggling learners?

When we start to apply the expectation of accountable conversation, it may slow down instruction, especially when students are just getting used to the procedure. Students often struggle as they try to master thinking independently and become responsible for their learning. This is especially true for upper elementary and secondary students. Many of our students have never been expected to participate in class discussions. Expect it to take some time for students to adjust and feel safe responding. You can also think of it as a step in classroom management; it can help turn the tide toward a more positive classroom culture!

We all feel the pressure of the ever-present climate of accountability. In this environment, it can be stressful to slow down the pace of instruction every time a student doesn't know the answer to a question. We might feel like we need to rush through the curriculum to make sure we "cover" everything required for the assessment test. When we do this, however, students often don't absorb the content that we are covering.

Even when we carefully monitor our pacing and thoughtfully plan the curriculum, we may struggle with effective ways to handle a student's requests for more information. One strategy that benefits students, keeps the pace of the lesson, and still provides support is Turn & Tell Five.

Here's how it works:
If a called-on student requests more information, tell the whole class to turn to the person next to them and discuss possible answers. Give students five seconds to speak to one another and exchange information.
Provide the same student who requested information an opportunity to respond.

Here is how it might sound in a typical classroom:

Second Grade Social Studies Dialogue
TURN & TELL FIVE

TEACHER Yesterday, we were learning about communities. What is one example of a community? Let's see...(Teacher draws Willie's name out of a stack of cards.) Willie?

WILLIE I forgot.

TEACHER Can you use the strategy we talked about earlier? Remember the poster?

WILLIE Oh yeah. Can I please have some more information?

TEACHER Sure, Willie. Everyone turn to your partners and, on "Go," give an example of a community. You have five seconds; I'm going to count down with my fingers. Ready, go. (Teacher uses fingers to count from five to one, then speaks to Willie directly.) Willie, are you ready?

WILLIE Yeah.

TEACHER Okay, everybody, eyes on me. Willie, can you give me an example of a community?

WILLIE Yeah. Families are communities, right?

TEACHER Yes, great example! Let's see who will be picked to give me another example...

WATCH

Student Asking
to Repeat the
Question

"I am an educator who has had the great fortune of starting my career already utilizing the concepts from *7 Steps to a Language-Rich, Interactive Classroom*. This concept has helped me to reach and develop my EL students in an amazing way. The students who are used to remaining quiet have nowhere to hide in my classroom, but they feel safe and supported enough to answer when randomly called on. I continue to advocate for the 7 Steps on my campus, and for my district."

**Christopher Hurst, Social Studies Teacher
White Oak Middle School, New Caney ISD**

(9) **How does Step 1 promote language acquisition for MLLs?**

Step 1 provides multilingual learners (MLLs) with a clear path to finding information when they are unsure in class. The various options for "What to Say Instead of I Don't Know" give them the language needed to advocate for themselves. This creates an environment where students are comfortable in responding to questions even when they do not know the answer…yet.

When working with MLLs, adding visuals for each alternative to "I don't know" will increase students' understanding of the questions.

For example:

May I please have more time?

 May I ask a friend?

To use the strategy in class, ensure the options are visible to all students and easy for the teacher to reference. Introduce and chorally read the "What to Say Instead of I Don't Know" options with the class, then model what will happen when the teacher asks a question that the student doesn't know the answer to. Stay positive and patient, referring frequently to the questions and coaching students on how to use them.

How do I implement Step 1 in a virtual environment?

One way teachers have been implementing this step when teaching students online has been to post an image of the choices of "What to Say Instead of I Don't Know" as a virtual background. Another possibility is to place a poster in a position visible to the students so that we can refer to it while teaching. For older students who have a notebook or spiral for the class, have them write the "What to Say Instead of I Don't Know" options inside the front cover, where they can find them quickly. When students are unable to respond, we can also chat with them privately to give them strategies that allow them to respond to questions.

Some teachers use a specific strategy that is helpful when it is unclear whether lack of response is a technical issue or the student is choosing not to respond. We can let the student know we will have them respond at a later time by saying something like, "It looks like we are having some issues. I'm going to follow up during asynchronous/independent time."

Chat
From Me to Julieta Arroyo **(Private):** Can you ask Chloe again now and see what she says? (Step #1 - What to say when you don't know what to say) You can also ask students to repeat another student's idea (Example: Esteban repeats or rephrases Liam's idea)
From Me to Everyone: Liam, you used great details from the text to analyze.
From Liam Mendez to Everyone: Thank you!
From Me to Everyone: Jorge, great analysis!
To: Everyone ☐ File ⋯ Type message here...

- ☐ Post the "What to Say Instead of I Don't Know" choices as part of a virtual background.
- ☐ Have the poster or another image of the choices visible from multiple angles.
- ☐ Offer wait time and a follow-up opportunity during asynchronous instruction.
- ☐ Have small, post-it sized "Instead of IDK" posters for the students' desks at home. Tape these in a journal, on the desk, or on a laptop.
- ☐ Pre-plan slides with key questions to include a "What to say instead of IDK" box in the corner. Copy and paste these boxes into any slide with a question.
- ☐ Focus on two to three "IDK" phrases each week and post in the corner with objectives. Allow students to collect, create their own, etc.

NOTES FROM THE FIELD

"I just observed a teacher in a face-to-face room setting this up as a page in the virtual notebook with the students. A student suggested adding, 'Could you please restate the question?' to the list, and the teacher typed it up. That was a grade four ELA classroom, and the students did all the activities in the virtual notebook on Chromebooks."

- Natalia Heckmann

Have students speak in complete sentences.

Meet Natalie. She is an eighth-grader in a U.S. History class. The teacher calls on Natalie and asks her to summarize what the class just read. Natalie thinks for a moment and then responds:

"Ok, now, there were the British ones… and the other ones…and they didn't like each other, with the taxation representation thingy…and they were all throwing tea into the water and were mad and stuff and wanted, you know… independence and everything. They called it a tea party, but they didn't have no balloons or nothing."

Any eighth-grade teacher knows that this kind of response is all too common. Presumably, when Natalie writes her thoughts on paper, she will write in much the same way. This is understandable, as it's very hard for students to write in a way they do not speak. If we want students to use formal academic language in their speaking and writing, we need to teach them how to communicate using formal academic language. The first step is to learn how to thoroughly express one's thoughts using complete sentences. We, teachers, can facilitate this first step by establishing the expectation that students respond in complete sentences.

This simple expectation dramatically improves the quality of interactions in our classrooms. When we encourage our students to use complete sentences, they learn to think in complete thoughts. They link new words to new concepts and can practice using more complex language structures.

Now, not every single interaction in the classroom between the teacher and the students, or among students, requires complete sentences; sometimes, informal language is appropriate, even in professional settings. However, students must have frequent experiences using formal language; thus, it is critical to provide ample opportunities in class that require them to use complete sentences. In doing so, students learn how to develop their thoughts and use formal language structures, both orally and in writing.

By providing students with opportunities to communicate while holding them accountable for using complete sentences, we may be giving them a passport to clear communication in both the academic and professional worlds.

Here's how it might sound in a typical classroom:

Fifth Grade Math Dialogue
COMPLETE SENTENCES

TEACHER We've been looking at fractions and talking about how to add them. What was the first step in adding two fractions? *(Teacher draws Baljeet's name from a stack.)* Baljeet?

BALJEET The first step in adding fractions is to find a common denominator.

TEACHER Exactly. When we look at these two fractions, one fourth and one third, what would the common denominator be? *(Teacher draws Aisha's name from a stack.)* Aisha?

AISHA Twelve.

TEACHER *(Smiling and using a supportive tone.)* Could I have that in a sentence, please?

AISHA The common denominator of three and four is twelve.

TEACHER Thanks, Aisha. How did Aisha find the common denominator? *(Teacher draws Enrique's name from a stack.)* Enrique? How do you think Aisha found the common denominator?

ENRIQUE With three and four. *(Teacher waits a moment, and Enrique rephrases his answer.)* I mean, Aisha found the common denominator by multiplying three and four.

One way to support students as they learn to respond with complete sentences is to provide them with sentence stems. A sentence stem is a short phrase that gives students the beginning, or the frame, of a sentence that helps them structure a response. Using sentence stems dramatically changes the quality and tone of a classroom because it helps students become increasingly more comfortable using academic language for expression.

WATCH

Student-to-student
Discussions Using
Complete Sentences

Here are some examples of sentence stems:

Question	Stem
Why does inertia have a considerable effect in this situation?	Inertia has a considerable effect in this situation because…
How would you calculate the volume of this cylinder?	To calculate the volume, I need to…
What is your opinion?	My opinion is…
How would you justify your answer?	I would justify my answer by…
What was the most damaging effect of the 1900 storm in Galveston?	The most damaging effect of the storm was_____ because…

"Over the course of the last 5 years, our teachers district-wide have received 7 Steps training. We recognize that ALL students benefit from instruction that consistently encourages them communicating their learning. As a result, we have observed more ownership in their learning and definitely more academic discourse between students/students and students/teachers."

Dr. Jennifer Valdez
Deputy Superintendent of Academics
Alvin ISD

WHAT RESEARCH SAYS

The National Literacy Panel on Language Minority Children and Youth (August & Shanahan, 2006) highlighted that there is a positive relationship between oral proficiency and reading and writing proficiency for English learners when teaching English acquisition skills. Studies also show that when students are proficient in oral language, they are more adept in their language skills and perform better on content-area assessments (de Araujo et al., 2018; Lesaux & Geva, 2006; Lara-Alecio et al., 2012). Calderón and Slakk (2018) promote the notion that students must practice using complete sentences to frame the words in the proper context for students to learn content vocabulary.

Donnelly and Roe (2010) pointed to developing sentence frames for oral-language practice as an effective approach for incorporating the language necessary for students to think, talk, and write about content concepts. Similarly, the research-based SIOP Model (Echevarria et al., 2017) demonstrates that students need frequent opportunities for interaction with content to encourage elaborated responses and build content mastery while developing language skills. Classroom cultures that promote the use of complete sentences routinely foster student elaboration, while instruction relying only on one-word responses to questions fails to maximize opportunities for students to engage in rich classroom conversation.

Prompting students to speak in complete sentences provides a means for students to hear content-area vocabulary used in context, not only by the teacher but also by their peers. Repeated use of targeted vocabulary while teaching complex content, particularly to English learners, will simultaneously help build students' written and oral language proficiency (Baker et al., 2014).

Step it UP!

*I*magine you have established a system of responding with complete sentences so well that you no longer need to prompt students to do so. That means you have given these students a "voice," which is an amazing accomplishment! Now you can STEP IT UP by encouraging students to elaborate on their ideas by adding more information and being proud of how well they can articulate a detailed response. This is also helpful because it is important to limit the amount of time we spend talking and encourage students to do most of the talking (and thinking!).

Building this type of confidence in students requires that they believe you will honor their responses for what they do know rather than what they do not yet understand. By praising the value of what they add to the lesson, you engage students in rich, content-appropriate responses. You begin by guiding them to richer responses through the use of scaffolding tools. These will refocus the students on the original question, refer to their positive feedback, and ask them to go just a little bit further by adding more information. This may evolve into using complex, compound sentences to respond to questions or add leading questions to their responses. The way you, as the teacher, respond can spur on more profound, more constructive, and more thoughtful feedback, which will encourage class discussions.

Here are examples of basic student responses and scaffolds to increase response complexity:

Student Sentence	Teacher Scaffold
√ The answer to the problem 2x + 14 = 28 is x=7	That's right! Can you take us through the steps you used to figure that out?
√ I don't think I got the right answer...	Tell us what you did first to try and figure it out or where you got stuck. And then...?
√ The life cycle of the butterfly has four stages.	Which stages show "metamorphosis," and how can you prove that?
√ The climax of the story is when grandma dies.	What rising action made you think this was the turning point of the story?
√ The cause of World War II was Germany and Hitler.	This is what many believe, but why do you think that is true?
√ I wrote my essay about my dog.	What type of writing style did you use, and who was your audience?

Frequently Asked Questions

1 **How can we encourage students to respond with more than just one simple sentence, especially when answering higher-level questions?**

We can encourage students to respond with more than a simple sentence at the factual level (e.g., "Five times twenty is one hundred") when we ask them questions at a more complex level. For example, we can ask a question regarding the process they used to arrive at the answer instead of asking for just the answer. We, as teachers, are often so focused on getting the students to the "right" answer that we sometimes forget to give them credit for the steps they took to get there! If students know that we consistently expect them to be ready to respond in complete sentences and to show their thinking and evidence, they will learn to contribute in ways that go beyond our expectations.

One way to bolster higher-level responses from students is to have them get in the habit of consistently citing evidence for their claims when responding to questions. The "Prove It" strategies encouraged by the National Paideia Center (2021) have students cite evidence with stems such as these:

» **"According to the text…"**
» **"According to the graph/map/legend…"**
» **"On page __, it says…"**
» **"I know this because…"**
» **"__ proves that…"**
» **"An example from the text is…"**

We can also use open-ended, higher-order questioning strategies based upon Bloom's taxonomy to develop our students' habits of thinking at higher levels and giving extended responses. Let's move beyond questions that focus exclusively on "right" answers and focus instead on developing students' capacity to analyze, evaluate, and create by asking deeper questions.

Here are some ideas for moving toward higher-order thinking questions:

Lower-level Question (Remember, Understand)	Higher-level Question (Apply, Analyze, Evaluate, Create)
What was one cause of the Civil War?	How did slavery contribute to the onset of the Civil War?
What's a2*a2?	Why are exponents added when bases are multiplied?
What is the purpose of a thesis statement?	Is this a good example of a thesis statement? Why or why not?
What is the powerhouse of the cell?	How do the mitochondria create chemical energy?

If done well, good questions can also create a classroom culture that welcomes differences when exploring answers to content-based questions. At this point, it is critical to let go of the reins on how questions are answered and allow students to use their own voices as they develop more in-depth responses. **Getting more than just one simple sentence is as much about the students' actions as it is about the teacher's.** Allowing students to respond from their own points of view will encourage diverse ways of thinking. It is not just about having an open-ended question; it is also about being open as a teacher to a variety of explanations, experiences, and points of view.

The following chart shows how we can move from common questions (for which we would expect a complete sentence) to better questions (where we would expect elaboration) to follow-up questions (where we are open to diverse explanations and points of view).

Common Questions	Better Question	Follow-up
What is the main idea of the story?	What actions in the story point readers to the main idea and plot?	Which part of the plot is the most exciting to you, and why?
What is the topic of your persuasive essay?	What writing tools did you use to try to persuade your audience?	How strongly do you believe in what you wrote? Why?
When was the attack on Fort Sumter?	How did President Lincoln respond to the attack on Fort Sumter?	Do you agree with Lincoln's response to the attack on Fort Sumter? Why?
What is the answer to 1/3 times 1/4?	How do you multiply 1/3 times 1/4?	If you were going to explain what is happening when you multiply fractions to someone who didn't understand, what images would you use, and why?
Why do humans have skeletons?	What do you think is the most important bone in the body? Why?	Why do you think a human skeleton might be symmetrical? What advantages do you think a symmetrical skeleton gives us?

2 **Will it strain classroom conversation and limit students' abilities to express themselves if we expect them to rephrase answers using complete sentences?**

No. Rather than limiting classroom conversation, the expectation of using complete sentences in the classroom actually enhances the free flow of ideas. Elaboration is rare in classrooms where one-word and short-phrase answers are the norms. In these situations, students do not hear other students regularly communicating with complete thoughts and sentences. Instead, they hear phrases and fragments in response to teacher questions. In contrast, when complete thoughts are the norm, students quickly become more comfortable elaborating and expressing their ideas. When students are asked open-ended questions at a higher level, they are able to say much more by using complete sentences.

We need to be careful, however, not to overdo the use of complete sentences in class. We want students to respond in complete sentences when we ask them questions directly during whole-class interactions, but we do not expect them to communicate with complete sentences in every single interaction. A simple guideline is to make sure that, when we're introducing a new question or topic in a discussion, we reiterate the expectation for using complete sentences. If we have an open discussion, we can relax and allow the free flow of ideas.

Here's how the interactions discussed just now might sound in a typical classroom:

12th Grade Government Dialogue:

BALANCING THE USE OF COMPLETE SENTENCES

TEACHER We've been talking about the tension between federal and state governments in the American system. What was one source of those problems? *(Teacher draws Finn's name out of a stack.)* Finn?

FINN The Constitution. *(Teacher pauses and glances at a poster that says, "Please express your thoughts in complete sentences.")* One source of the tension was the Constitution. Didn't it give powers to both groups?

TEACHER What do you mean?

FINN Both have some power. Like, the federal government can do some things and state governments can do other things.

TEACHER What kinds of things can the federal government do? *(Candace raises her hand.)*

CANDACE Control the foreign policy.

TEACHER Can you tell me more about that?

WATCH
Speaking in
Complete
Sentences

③ Do students with disabilities, multilingual learners, and students with limited or interrupted formal education (SLIFE) have to express themselves using complete sentences, too?

Yes! Unless a student has a disability–with an Individualized Education Plan (IEP) that indicates otherwise–expect all students to participate. With a few simple techniques, everyone can be included in this process.

Multilingual learners and SLIFE students often have to negotiate content and complex language structures simultaneously. When they are in a classroom with native speakers, providing them with extra support is essential. Giving sentence starters like, "The answer is…" and "I think…" improves communication abilities for students learning a new language. This technique eliminates juggling unfamiliar language structures, and it makes communication easier for students.

Another strategy when working with multilingual learners who are insecure about their pronunciation is to allow students to whisper complete sentences to you. You could then repeat what they said to the whole class. Doing this can make more reticent speakers feel safe, supported, and involved.

④ What if students refuse to respond using complete sentences?

When students are provided with an adequate rationale, most of them will come on board. Students need a reason to practice speaking in complete sentences in the classroom, and the reason has to make sense to them. One helpful method is to talk to students about the importance of sounding professional to achieve success in life. We can explain that using complex, formal language allows people to communicate clearly, express themselves completely, be understood, and understand others.

To underscore the importance of complete sentences, we have provided two examples below of a job interview that you can share with your students. Have students read and act out the two interviews. To bring out the fun in this activity, encourage students to add humor as they energetically demonstrate the differences between the two scenarios. Then ask students to decide which applicant they think will get the job and explain why. Discussing this scenario with students usually helps to create buy-in for the strategy. If students are still resistant to participation, talk to them individually to explain other sensible reasons for using the technique.

APPLICANT A

EMPLOYER So, tell me about your work experience.

APPLICANT Burger King.

EMPLOYER What did you do at Burger King?

APPLICANT The register, the grill, and the drive-through.

EMPLOYER Did you enjoy working there?

APPLICANT Yeah.

APPLICANT B

EMPLOYER So, tell me about your work experience.

APPLICANT My work experience includes working at Burger King.

EMPLOYER What did you do at Burger King?

APPLICANT While I was at Burger King, I worked at the register; I cooked on the grill, and I was also able to work in the drive-through sometimes.

EMPLOYER Did you enjoy working there?

APPLICANT Yes, I enjoyed it very much.

When should I introduce this strategy to my students?

It's always best to introduce the practice of using complete sentences at the beginning of the school year. Explain the expectation of accountable conversation with students first (see p. 25) and then explain how they are expected to participate in class discussions using complete sentences. Many teachers find implementation easier than they thought it would be once they've clearly communicated the goal and the expectations of the strategy to students.

How does Step 2 promote language acquisition for MLLs?

Step 2 can feel like a lofty goal, especially when you have newcomer multilingual learners in your classroom. Be not afraid; sentence stems are your friends! Sentence stems or sentence frames shift the cognitive load for MLLs when they're sharing ideas in a complete sentence. Their focus can move from how to begin their sentence and use correct grammar, to how they can meaningfully share their understanding.Giving the students the start to the sentence does not lessen their contribution to the content; rather, it provides an opportunity for students to practice grammatical structures and vocabulary while lowering their affective filters (emotional/psychological barriers to language acquisition). These sentence stems can be used during writing as well. Students cannot write in a way they cannot speak, so practicing speaking in complete sentences will improve students' writing as well.

General sentence stems can be used several times on a variety of topics; such as discussion stems or content specific stems that can be made permanently available to students on a poster, at their desks, on bookmarks, etc. General sentence stems give students the language to share their ideas, agree or disagree with others, ask questions, make connections between their own ideas and other students', and paraphrase or summarize content.

General ELA Stems

I predict...

I can infer___from...

The author states___which makes me think...

The text evidence on page__proves...

I can connect___to___because... (text to self, text to text, text to world)

General Math Stems

The first step to solving the problem is...

My answer is reasonable because...

The strategy I used to solve for _____ was...

I agree/disagree with _____'s answer because...

I learned...

General Science Stems

I observed...

The data/evidence shows...

The problem can be solved by...

The cause/effect of___ is...

Based on the data/evidence a conclusion I can make is...

This reminds me of...

General Social Studies Stems

I predict...

I can infer___because...

The similarities/differences between ____ and _____ are...

Evidence of _____ is shown in the (video, cartoon, reading) by...

The cause/effect of___was...

General Discussion Stems (All Content Areas)

I think...

I can infer...

I agree/disagree with _____ because...

I would like to add...

I can connect (reading, student idea, previous learning) to...

What I heard you say is...

These are examples for varying content areas, but they are by no means an exhaustive list. General sentence stems for your classroom may look different based on the content and grade level you teach.

Specific sentence stems can be added to slides, boards, or papers to help students answer a specific question. These are a great way to get extra practice with academic vocabulary. For example:

How do you find slope using a graph?
I can find slope using a graph by...

Many of us may remember being taught how to change a question into the beginning of an answer when we were in school. This is a lesson we can model for our students as well. Stems are a great scaffold to support students in their language learning, but we can empower students to create their own stems by showing them how to use the question as their sentence starter.

(7)

How do I implement
Step 2 in a
virtual environment?

When working with students in a virtual environment, it is still possible to have the students communicate using complete sentences. This can occur when students are sharing orally or when they are typing into a chat. To do this, we need to make sure sentence stems are visible to students and that they have access to the stems in breakout rooms or during asynchronous learning. We can also encourage students to elaborate on their thoughts when they give answers using single words or short phrases. For example, we can say something like, "That's a great idea, Felicity. Can you unmute and say that in a complete sentence?"

Some students, such as multilingual learners, may benefit from practicing pronunciation even when working in a virtual classroom. One way to do this is through choral response. We can ask the students to mute their microphones and then repeat after us. We can let them know that we are watching them on the screen to see if they are pronouncing the words.

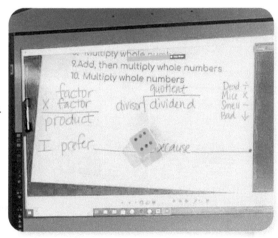

- ☐ Encourage the use of complete sentences in the chat.
- ☐ When students type something in the chat that is incomplete, solicit responses by saying something like, "That's a great idea. Can you unmute and say that in a complete sentence?"
- ☐ Alternate between writing in chat and unmuting/speaking out loud.
- ☐ Make sure sentence stems are visible to students and they have access to the stems in break-out rooms and during asynchronous learning. One option is to write the sentence stems in the presenter notes section below the slide. Make sure to set the "view" mode so students can see this notes section.
- ☐ Use choral response, and have students clearly say the words even though they are on mute. Tell them that you are using an "honor system," and you trust them to say the words clearly.
- ☐ Use a color-coded system within your presentations to help students access sentence stems. For example, all sentence stems will be blue throughout the year so they're easily noticed. Perhaps change the color when students are speaking.
- ☐ Post a sentence stem on a slide, and have students finish the stem in the chat. Randomly call on students to respond in a complete sentence, combining both the posted stem and their response.

Randomize and rotate when calling on students.

As teachers, we often struggle with having the same few students always raise their hands to respond to questions as the rest of the class sits quietly. We often end up calling on these energetic participators because they usually seem to know the answer, and doing so allows us to maintain the pace of our lesson. Every so often, when we insist that other students respond, we are met with frustration, anxiety, or blank stares. There are better ways to encourage hesitant or disengaged students to respond during whole-class instruction: randomizing and rotating responses when calling on students.

When teachers expect all students to contribute, the culture of the classroom changes. Students pay closer attention, knowing they might be called on at any moment. This creates a variety of responses, often stimulating further discussion in the process of learning new material–which is a great way to learn! Teachers benefit from using a system of randomization and rotation, and students are also encouraged when they believe their teacher has complete confidence that the students can add value to the lesson. Another benefit is that students begin to realize that taking risks to further develop learning is always met with support and is simply part of how the classroom works. Strong implementation of this step is key to building a whole-class 7 Steps lesson structure that supports all levels of learners.

Randomizing

Randomizing is one effective way to meet this goal and ensure total class participation. It requires very little planning: simply create a bank of names, such as index cards or Popsicle® sticks with each student's name, and randomly pull from that bank when calling on students.

When randomizing, avoid asking questions that begin with phrases like this:

"Who can tell me..."
"Let's see who knows..."
"Does anyone know..."
"Can someone tell the class..."

These phrases typically encourage the students who are already participating and who shout out and dominate discussion to continue to do so. However, our goal is to have everyone involved in discussions so we can assess all students' understanding of concepts, not just those who enjoy actively participating. When we do not use random selection to assess students, we only check the comprehension of a few highly motivated students.

When randomizing, the questioning technique looks like this:

1. Ask the question.
It is important to ask the questions without soliciting volunteers. It may even help to ask students explicitly not to raise their hands; this eliminates the temptation to call only on those who volunteer.

2. Pause.
Pausing after the question gives everyone a chance to think, creating some positive tension as students wonder who the teacher will call on.

3. Select a student to respond using a random selection system.
Having an established random selection system (e.g., drawing an index card from a pile) ensures that all students are paying attention and have a fair chance to be called on to respond.

Using randomization promotes higher student engagement and a more accurate assessment of student understanding. With this method, students grow accustomed to always being prepared to respond, and we grow more accustomed to fostering total class participation.

Rotating

In some classroom discussions, using a rotation strategy rather than a randomizing strategy may provide an even greater opportunity for participation. Spencer Kagan's time-tested Numbered Heads Together (1992) is an easy way to get everyone involved and continue to avoid the problems of calling on the same students again and again. Numbered Heads Together works best with open-ended questions that have more than one possible response. Of course, all students should share their answers in complete sentences.

Some other ways to facilitate randomizing or rotating include marking a seating chart as students are called on, numbering desks, and using online randomizers to select student names. The important thing is not which system we use, but that we have a system in place. It is crucial to include everyone. Without a system, total participation is not guaranteed.

There are times when it may be helpful to have an open dialogue without using index cards or seating charts. Sometimes, teachers may like the energy of students calling out answers and freely exchanging ideas. These discussions can be positive experiences, but we have to be careful because some students may not always feel like they are a part of the discussion. If we do not have a system in place that includes everyone, students will be left out. Those students are often at-risk learners, students with special needs, and multilingual learners, all of whom would most benefit from active participation.

Steps for Numbered Heads Together

1. Divide students into groups of four.

2. Ask students to count off within the group (one through four) so each has a number.

3. Ask a question.

4. Give groups a chance to talk to each other about the answer.

5. Randomly select a number, one through four.

6. Ask the person in each group that has that number to stand up: "The person who is number __, please stand."

7. Have the person whose number was selected report for the group.

8. If a group has the same response as another group, instruct students to respond with this sentence stem: "We agree that __ because..."

9. Repeat the procedure with other questions until all students have had an opportunity to speak for their groups.

Use index cards: Record each student's name on an index card. Draw one of the index cards from the stack, and ask that student to respond to a given question.

Organize Numbered Heads Together: Place students in groups of 4 or 5. Have each group member number off from 1–5, explaining that the number they used in the count off will be their number for the remainder of the day. Ask a question, and then randomly select one of the numbers. All students who have that number respond (Kagan, 1992).

Hold a deck of cards: Hand out one card to each student, then randomize by calling any of the following: red, black, spades, hearts, diamonds, clubs, face cards, certain numbers, etc.

Designate categories: Assign a category to individual students or tables of students, such as: parts of speech, days of the week, names of planets, or names of historical figures, etc.

Place colored stickers on desks: Place an assortment of colored stickers randomly on student desks. Ask all the reds, yellows, blues, or greens to respond to questions.

Use individual characteristics: Provide a starting point for randomizing and rotating, such as personal characteristics like hair color, type of shoes, or color of shirt for students to respond to questions.

Scan the class roster or grade book: Choose students at random from the list in the class roster or grade book.

WHAT RESEARCH SAYS

Student engagement is highly correlated to student achievement. Schmoker (2018) and Gunuc (2014) showed that learning increases when students are focused on tasks during instruction and that significant relationships exist between students' academic achievement and cognitive student engagement. A meta-analysis of research showed that highly engaged students do more than just attend to the lessons; they put forth persistent effort, self-regulate their academic goals, challenge themselves to succeed, and enjoy learning (Christenson et al., 2012). Even in higher education, students who attended lectures where teachers used random questioning reported that they were far more likely to be engaged than in classes without random questioning. The author surmised that random questioning increases student preparedness, attentiveness, and achievement (Brooks et al., 2014).

During the collection of observational data on the 7 Steps methodology (Goldman et al., 2021), there was substantial evidence that randomizing and rotating responses is particularly helpful in maintaining accountability during whole-class instruction and cooperative tasks. The data also pointed to the notion that maintaining student engagement through the use of this strategy promotes a classroom implementation system that includes the use of the previous strategic Steps 1 and 2, thereby supporting English learners at multiple levels.

Step it UP!

Once you have helped students become comfortable responding when randomly called upon, to STEP IT UP, start structuring student-to-student conversations in ways that incorporate randomizing and rotating. This will result in richer conversations requiring all students to get in the habit of including everyone in their discussions. Several strategies and discussion structures allow all students to participate, such as Lines of Communication, Carousel, Fold the Line, and Inside/Outside Circles (see p. 41).

One beneficial structure that engages students in creating more focused responses while listening carefully to all of their peers is a technique called Talking Chips. When using Talking Chips, the teacher places students into discussion groups and gives the same number of index cards with sentence stems to every student. The teacher then gives a topic for discussion or asks a question. Each student must respond using one of the stems, discarding the index card after speaking. Students who run out of cards cannot talk anymore. The discussion continues until all members of the group have used all of their cards.

To encourage higher-order thinking using this structure, teachers can use stems similar to these on the cards:

A different idea is...

I agree with_____ because...

I respectfully disagree. On the contrary...

The evidence for_____ is...

_____ 's point is important because...

Adding to what_____said, ...

Overall, my main point is...

I agree with _____ , but we also have to consider...

This activity can also be done virtually by posting a question or discussion topic in an online forum or collaboration board and using virtual "chips" or images of tokens moved from one place to another to signify students taking turns speaking. Students could also respond synchronously or asynchronously by replying to the question and responding to two other student's comments.

WATCH
Rotating partners/
Grouping patterns

Frequently Asked Questions

1 Why should I use randomization during open-ended student-to-student conversations? What would that look like?

Higher-level questions open to a variety of responses provide opportunities for students to share their thoughts from unique perspectives. In learning environments with students from various cultures and socio-economic backgrounds, providing opportunities for students to reflectively hear every other student's point of view can help build a sense of community in the classroom.

Many partner and grouping strategies promote discussion among all students. However, it's important that these discussions get students to use critical and creative thinking skills and learn to listen to their conversation partners. It helps if we ask open-ended, higher-level questions when using techniques that involve students talking with multiple conversation partners.

The following structures in some way involve randomizing and rotating to make sure all students participate in open-ended, small-group discussions:

Lines of Communication: Students form two lines facing one another. The students in each line share ideas, review concepts, or ask one another questions. After the first discussion, one row moves, and the other row remains stationary so that each student now has a new partner (Dutro & Smith, 2015).

Carousel: The teacher posts questions in various stations around the room, then assigns students to groups and each group to a station. Students have a specified time to answer the questions at each station, and groups rotate around the room until everyone answers all questions.

Fold the Line: Students line up chronologically based on a predetermined characteristic such as height, age, number of pets, etc. The line then folds in half upon itself, providing each student with a partner. Partners then respond to a given task or question (Kagan, 1992).

Inside/Outside Circle: Students form two concentric circles facing one another—an inside circle and an outside circle. Students then participate in a short, guided discussion or review with their partners. After the discussion, the outside circle rotates to the right while the inside circle remains still. Each student now has a new partner for discussion (Kagan, 1992).

Gallery Walk: The teacher posts questions, prompts, or tasks in various stations around the room and gives a specified time to answer the question or complete the task at each station. Students then rotate around the room until each has visited every station.

"Step 3 allows for ALL students to be held accountable for learning and having a voice in the classroom. As the book states, asking questions without solicitation of volunteers helps the teacher not always call on those who raise their hand first. For students, the pause causes 'positive tension' and engagement as they wait to see who will share. Additionally, they grow accustomed to always being prepared to respond."

Jordan Greer
ESL Language Coach, Pre-K-5th Grade
McSpedden Elementary, Frisco ISD

 ## How often should we use randomizing and rotating for calling on students?

While it is unnecessary to randomize for every single question, frequent use of this strategy can greatly benefit all students. A helpful guideline is to call on students randomly whenever there is a whole-class discussion on a new question or a new topic. Other kinds of questioning are effective for motivating students, getting new ideas on the table, creating resources, and generating creative energy. But, if we want to check for understanding and ensure equity, we must frequently randomize, or rotate, whom we select to respond to questions. Once we have opened up a discussion and assessed the comprehension of one or more non-volunteers, it's all right to have other students volunteer ideas. If we want to generate a flow of ideas on a topic after using random selection, we can open the class discussion to all.

 ## What should we do about students who blurt out answers?

Teaching students to refrain from blurting out answers is worth the time and effort. A good starting point is to explain to students why we want them to avoid calling out answers. For elementary classrooms, setting up a role-play with two students having a conversation and a third student who constantly interrupts provides a clear example for students. After watching this role-play, ask students what they think of the interruptions and have them write their responses. Most students will describe such behavior as impolite, unkind, immature, etc. Explain that when we call on a student by name, we have begun a conversation. If others choose to talk over the conversation, that is an example of interrupting, and is not considered a constructive addition to the conversation.

In secondary classrooms, it is unrealistic to tell students they can never talk without raising their hands. This is not the way academic discourse usually takes place among adults in professional and university settings. There are some types of discussion where raising hands or waiting for the speaker to call on someone inhibits the free flow of ideas. Explain that, to maintain a respectful classroom culture, we want students to avoid calling out and interrupting others on these three occasions:

» **When we are using a randomizing system**

» **When we call on another student by name**

» **When another student has not finished expressing ideas**

Most students see these guidelines as reasonable and agree that they build a safer classroom environment in which to answer questions and express views. Establishing these guidelines early in the year and enforcing them consistently is critical to their success.

(4) **Should we place the index cards and Popsicle® sticks back in the stack, or should we take them out as they're used to make sure everyone gets a chance to respond?**

Different teachers have different answers to this question. Some students know they will no longer be called on when their stick or card is removed, and they check out of the

1. Return the cards to the bottom of the stack.

2. Draw mostly from the top half of the stack, occasionally drawing from the bottom so student names have the potential of occurring again.

3. Use a "double bucket" for the sticks. Start with everyone's stick in the outside bucket, and move them to the inside bucket after being drawn.

4. Draw mainly from the outside bucket during discussions, but occasionally draw from the inside bucket as well.

discussion. This problem can be solved in a few ways:Combine randomizing and rotating. During a discussion using Numbered Heads together, call on all the "number two" students to share. Afterward, randomly call on a student to respond to what was shared by person number two, using the sentence stems, "I agree with ____ that …" or "I disagree with ____ that…"

(5) **What about students who are way behind their peers? Won't it embarrass them if we call on them?**

Teaching students what to say when they don't know the answer (Step 1, p. 13) solves this problem. Students can feel confident when called on because even if they do not have the answer, they always have an appropriate response, such as, "May I please have some more information?"

WATCH
Popsicle® Sticks
in Math Class

6. Will it discourage students who want to share if I randomize and rotate responses? Will they stop wanting to participate if I redirect them when they blurt out answers?

Students who like to talk and share in class are sometimes frustrated at the beginning when they can no longer be the center of the teacher's attention. Many students are used to dominating classroom discussions and tie their sense of self-worth to their ability to answer questions and share thoughts. Sometimes these students will complain about the use of randomization techniques. When we use a strategy like Numbered Heads Together, these students have a chance to be heard by others in their group. These kinds of interactive techniques meet the needs of these students.

An additional benefit of randomizing and rotating responses is that students learn to listen actively to one another. Sometimes students who dominate discussions do not realize that other students who are quieter, or less verbal, have great ideas to share. By giving them a chance to slow down and hear what other students have to say, they learn both patience and tolerance for another student's point-of-view. The students who do not often share in discussions learn that their views are valuable and that they can successfully contribute to a healthy exchange of ideas, which forms the foundation for building argumentative literacy.

7. How does Step 3 promote language acquisition for MLLs?

Some MLLs cope with the challenge of learning a new language or the stress from adapting to a new culture by sitting quietly and disappearing into the background of the classroom. This is a self-preservation strategy, but it keeps the students from engaging in the content, and it keeps the teachers unaware of the students' gaps in understanding. On the surface, randomizing and rotating strategies may feel like we are raising the affective filter for MLLs; however, when we combine these strategies with total response signals, wait time, sentence stems, and group check-ins, they keep students engaged and create positive tension.

When using randomizing and rotating strategies with MLLs, ensure you provide think time for students as well as a total response signal they can use to indicate when they are ready. Always allow time for all students to formulate an answer, either individually or in small groups, prior to calling out a name. If the students know who will be called on before the teacher asks the question, they will check out and wait for the one student whose name was called.

"We have spent a lot of time discussing holding students accountable; therefore, Step 3, Randomizing & Rotating is one we always recommend as a priority. Our EL Coaches have developed instructional coaching tools when they observe teachers to help them track data on what students they call on."

Dr. Yolanda Rios,
Director of Multilingual/Title III/Migrant,
New Caney ISD

(8)

**How do I implement
Step 3 in a
virtual environment?**

Randomizing is just as important in virtual instruction as it is in face-to-face learning. After randomly selecting students, teachers can have them share their responses in the chat or aloud. Keep in mind that students may take time to get used to unmuting their microphones when they are randomly selected to speak.

Some of the same techniques listed above work virtually just as they do in class. For example, some teachers still use Popsicle® sticks and index cards to select students. Teachers can also use Numbered Heads Together (see p. 38) by having the students number off when they have discussions in breakout rooms. Many teachers use specific interactive apps and online platforms to select students randomly to respond to questions.

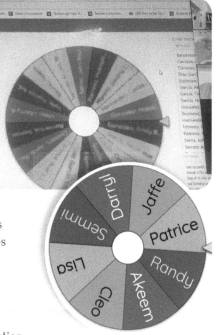

☐ Use online/digital apps or online platforms for randomization.

☐ Count people on the screen, then use dice to select a number randomly.

☐ Assign letters/numbers for students to determine in which order they will speak in breakout rooms. You can use these letters/numbers to share when all students return from the breakout rooms.

☐ Count off to a random number (i.e., the third student or the fifth student) on the participant list or a screenshot of students in the chat.

☐ Show a roster on the screen with numbers next to each student. Use numbered Popsicle® sticks to select a student randomly.

☐ Use clothing and other observable things on the screen to call on students; for example, "anyone wearing a black shirt."

Step 4

Use total response signals to check for understanding.

otal response signals are cues students can use to indicate they are ready to respond to a question or move on to new material. Response signals allow students to prepare for and participate in oral or written tasks in a nonthreatening way, and they provide a very effective tool for gauging student understanding in real time. There are three elements of an effective total response signal:

Total: Total response signals include every student in the classroom: at-risk learners, ELs, students with special needs, gifted students, and students with limited or interrupted formal education (SLIFE). Total means everyone.

Response: Every student will think through their response. After the teacher poses a question, students are given an opportunity to gather their thoughts and decide when they are ready to respond.

Signal: Once students are prepared to respond, they provide a signal, which must be clear enough so that teachers can immediately survey who is ready to respond.

Here's how it might sound in a typical classroom:

First Grade Social Studies Dialogue
TOTAL RESPONSE SIGNALS

TEACHER Okay, everyone, take a look at the map of our school on your desks. Show me thumbs-up as soon as you can find the principal's office. *(Students begin to put their thumbs up as they find the principal's office. The teacher notices a few students who have not put their thumbs up. This indicates they are struggling, so she walks to their desks and points out the location of the principal's office with her finger. These students put their thumbs up.)* Okay, I see everyone has found the principal's office. Now, I'm going to give you a sentence starter, and I'm going to select someone to form a sentence using the sentence starter. "The principal's office is next to..." *(Teacher selects a Popsicle® stick from the bucket.)* Felicia?

FELICIA The principal's office is next to the water fountain.

TEACHER Thanks, Felicia. Now, everyone, find the compass on your school map. It looks like this picture on the board. Show me a thumbs-up when you can find it.

In addition to showing student readiness, total response signals enable us to check consistently for student understanding. Think of them as instant, ongoing assessments used throughout a lesson. With response signals, we don't have to wait for the quiz, test, worksheet, or writing assignment to determine how well our students understand a topic. Instead, we can immediately check for understanding and see who is ready to move on, and who still needs help. There are four basic types of response signals:

Written Response: Students write their responses on paper, sticky notes, cards, whiteboards, or chalkboards and hold them up so they are visible to the teacher.

Ready Response: Students show they have finished a task or are ready to begin a new one. For example, in Thinker's Chin, students keep their hands on their chins until they finish thinking and are ready to respond to a question. When students remove their hands from their chins, that means they are ready.

Making Choices: Students show their response to a specific set of choices using a physical object or signal. For example, when reviewing for a multiple-choice test, give students letter cards labeled A, B, C, and D. After reading a question, ask students to show the card corresponding to their choice. We can instantly see how students respond to each question.

Ranking: Students show their relative agreement or disagreement with particular statements. For example, ask students if they agree or disagree with the following: "We should make a table before setting up an equation to solve this problem." Have students hold up a number on a scale of 1-5 to signal their level of agreement (5 = Strongly Agree, 4 = Agree, 3 = Undecided, 2 = Disagree, 1 = Strongly Disagree). Ask students to be ready to explain their reasoning.

WATCH
Physical
Response to
Show Readiness

The chart below gives specific examples of each type of response signal.

Written Response	• Hold up paper/notebook • Whiteboards • Personal chalkboards • Answers on index cards
Ready Response	• Hands up when ready • Hands down when ready • Thinker's Chin (hand off chin when ready) • Stand when ready • Sit when ready • Put your pen on your paper when ready to write • Put your pen down when finished writing • All eyes on teacher • Heads down

Making Choices	• Open hand/closed hand • Thumbs up/thumbs down • Pens up/pens down • Number wheels • Green card/red card • Move to the corner that you agree/disagree with • Letter/number choice cards: A, B, C, D or 1, 2, 3, 4
Ranking	• Rank with your fingers • Line up according to response • Knocking/clapping/cheering

"7 Steps is our sheltered instruction model here in Hays CISD. Our teachers love implementing the 7 Steps because they can see positive results instantly through increased engagement."

Sara Sparks,
ESL Specialist
Hays CISD

WHAT RESEARCH SAYS

Research indicates that student engagement improves attentiveness in the classroom, which results in increased student achievement (Jensen, 2005; Gunuc & Kuzu, 2015). Active response signals are a powerful way to get students' attention because they connect physical movement with mental processes. Christenson et al. (2012) identify classroom strategies that promote the use of active student responses to improve the quality of teaching and enhance student outcomes. Other research highlights evidence that students engaged in active response signals perform better on follow-up quizzes, tests, and the application of learned content knowledge (Randolph, 2007). Further studies show that teachers could easily implement active student response strategies that increase classroom participation, on-task behavior, and accurate responses over more traditional methods to elicit student engagement (Tincani & Tyman, 2016). Response signals significantly affect achievement for inner-city students during whole-class science instruction (Gardner et al., 1994) and for special needs students during whole-class math instruction (Christle & Schuster, 2003).

Specific response signals that have been frequently reviewed include response cards, choral response, and guided notes, which all yield findings that show students significantly outperform control groups that do not have active student response options. When students have increased opportunities to respond through methods like response cards, they are more engaged in active participation in the instruction than students participating by traditional hand-raising (Didion et al., 2020; Twyman & Heward, 2018). These response signals are also noted across current literature to be extremely effective measures for teachers to informally assess where their students are in content comprehension, enabling them to differentiate and better meet individual student needs.

Step it UP!

*T*otal response signals give you the opportunity to check in with everyone at the same time, and they also let the class know you won't leave anyone behind. To STEP IT UP, start strategically including total response signals to engage students at a higher level.

Some response signals measure student readiness (e.g., stand up if you are ready, put your pen on the desk when done answering, etc.). Some require students to show agreement or disagreement, and others require students to make a choice or even write out a thoughtful response. Each of these engages students at different levels of thinking. The written and ranking responses require a little more thinking to execute well. Targeting total response signals to specific levels of thinking (both lower-level and higher-level) can give valuable feedback about the students' understanding.

For example, compare the first two lower-order thinking signals below to the rest of the signals requiring higher-order thinking:

Total Response Signal	Levels of Thinking
Hand on your head when ready to answer a question	Remember, understand (lower-order)
Thumbs up if ready to respond; sideways if you need time	Understand, apply (lower-order)
Finger pointing to ear when you need more information	Understand, analyze (higher-order)
Number of fingers to show confidence in response	Understand, analyze (higher-order)
Hold up a number or letter to share the opinion you agree with	Analyze, evaluate (higher-order)
Stand back-to-back with your shoulder buddy once you've decided whose answer is best	Apply, analyze, evaluate (higher-order)
Move to a corner to discuss your choice/preference	Apply, analyze, evaluate (higher-order)
Hand to mouth like a microphone when ready to prove your answer	Evaluate, create (higher-order)

Frequently Asked Questions

 How can I encourage students to think at higher levels when they use total response signals?

It is helpful for us as teachers to think through which response signals we will use strategically throughout a lesson. For example, a multiple-choice activity will call for different response signals than an activity where students share written opinions or cite text evidence. We can use specific signals to move toward incorporating higher-order thinking and processing skills into various classroom activities.

The chart below can serve as a guide to help think through which response signals might be appropriate for various classroom applications. Notice how the levels of student thinking vary for different classroom activities and signals.

Classroom Activities	Total Response Signals	Thinking Skills
Ready to learn, completing a task, being prepared to proceed	Ready responses	Remember, understand
Understanding vocabulary, responding to a question, showing agreement or disagreement	Making choices	Remember, understand, apply
Showing level of agreement/disagreement, showing level of comprehension	Ranking	Analyze, evaluate
Giving opinions, citing evidence, showing work	Sharing written responses	Understand, apply, evaluate
Sharing personal understanding of a concept, linking key concepts and ideas together	Creating and sharing a visual/illustration	Apply, analyze, create

2 **How do you make sure students use response signals correctly? Won't many of them show a signal even though they're not ready just because all the other students are showing one?**

This can be a problem if we aren't intentional about how we use total response signals. It is crucial to structure the use of response signals so that students are relaxed and honest when they use them. We also have to be respectful and encouraging when students do not show us a signal. If we ask students to raise their hands when they are ready to respond, and many students still have their hands down, we must be supportive and assume they would raise their hands if they had a response. At this point, we can rephrase the question or ask everyone to put their hands down, clarify the information, and then ask the question again.

Varying the method of student response after a response signal helps students participate authentically. Sometimes students can share their thoughts with each other; other times, we might randomly select a student to share with the class. If we always have students share with each other after giving us a response signal, many will show signals even though they are not ready to respond; they know they can rely on their partners for ideas. Randomizing immediately after a response signal reduces this tendency.

This is how the situation might sound in a typical classroom:

Sixth Grade Language Arts Dialogue

HOLDING STUDENTS ACCOUNTABLE FOR THE USE OF TOTAL RESPONSE SIGNALS

TEACHER Okay, what do you think Stanley's motive was for leaving home? Raise your hand as soon as you have thought about a reason for Stanley to leave. *(All students raise their hands. Teacher randomly selects Leo's name from the stack of cards.)* Leo, what do you think?

LEO May I please have some more information?

TEACHER I think maybe the directions I gave weren't clear. Let me try again. Okay, class, raise your hand as soon as you have an answer. Please don't raise your hand until you are ready to respond. That way, I can make sure everybody's ready before I call on someone. *(Most students raise their hands. Some are still not raised.)*

TEACHER Okay, everyone, go ahead and put your hands down. Let's talk about motive again. Motive is the reason you do something. Think about what we read yesterday. Remember when Stanley left home? What do you think is his reason for leaving? Raise your hand when you can finish this sentence: "I think Stanley's motive for leaving was___." *(All students raise their hands.)* Leo, what do you think?

LEO Stanley's motive for leaving was that he thought everyone was mad at him.

(3) **What if students still won't show a response signal, even after being given ample time?**

If students do not show a response signal after ample time is given, ask everyone to put their hands down or stop showing a signal. Then clarify the concept, the question, or the instructions. Next, try to find out if anyone still needs help and give students a chance to clarify misunderstandings with someone sitting near them. Then, ask students once again to give the response signal. If there are still a few students who don't understand, we might work with them individually or ask if they understand what they've been instructed to do. Sometimes we may think decisions and tasks are easier than they are for our students. If more than two students delay too long in showing a response signal, we might need to think about how well students really understand the task or concept. One purpose of a response signal is to assess student understanding. If students are indicating to us that they don't understand something through the use of a response signal, then the signal is working well. The lack of response signals tells us where we need to reteach and refocus our instruction.

(4) **Won't students just look to see what other students' signals or answers are and then copy those responses?**

Yes, many students will do that. However, there are some strategies teachers can use to overcome this problem. One strategy to eliminate mimicking when using letter cards is to print the letters on one side only; another is to have students sit in rows or at tables that are organized so they cannot easily see how other students respond. Another alternative is to ask students to show their choices on a count of three, or when we say "Go."

As students begin trusting that the signals will help the teacher support them when they do not understand and find out what they think about various ideas, they will start showing their understanding and choices with the signals.

⑤ What about students with special needs who cannot use certain signals?

We need to be sensitive to what our students are physically capable of doing, and we have to avoid putting students in awkward situations by choosing to use total response signals they cannot complete. If a student has limited mobility and the response signal involves moving around the room, we want to give that student other options to express choice. If a student's level of cognitive development limits understanding or choices, we may need to modify or clarify our questions and procedures in such a way that special needs students can participate in the conversation meaningfully.

⑥ How does Step 4 promote language acquisition for MLLs?

Total response signals help lower the affective filter for MLLs by providing them with nonverbal ways to show readiness, choice, or ranking. Teachers can help even further by modeling the expectation for students. For example, if you are asking them to turn their paper over when they are ready, then model turning a paper over for your students to see. Teachers should keep in mind that language learners may need extra time to process the information and show their signals. During this processing time, try not to add information or restate the question. When we do this we are giving students even more information to process. However, if students have not given an answer in a significant amount of time, then restating the question or providing guiding questions may be helpful.

NOTES *FROM THE* FIELD

"I saw a teacher using what could be called a 'virtual whiteboard.' Each student had an individual, virtual space on which to write. The teacher was able to show all student responses on the screen at one time. This can be used as a formative assessment tool." - *Marcy Voss*

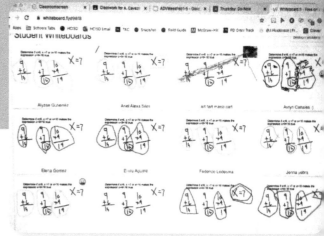

How do I implement
Step 4 in a
virtual environment?

Implementing Step 4 in a virtual environment is very similar to implementing it in face-to-face instruction. Some techniques found in the chart on p. 48, such as thumbs up/thumbs down and ranking with your fingers, work the same in virtual and non-virtual spaces. A virtual environment does present unique opportunities for response signals as well. You can refer to the following visual to see many examples that teachers can use in virtual learning.

☐ Tell students to unmute when they're ready to share. Alternatively, you can have students turn their cameras off and then on or cover the camera with their hands and then uncover it when they are ready to share.

☐ Ask students to show a reaction when they're ready to share (applause, heart, raised hand).

☐ Have students type in the chat or an interactive app. For more shy students you can adjust the settings in most platforms so that the students can reply just to you in the chat instead of to everyone publicly.

☐ Ask students to apply a background effect or filter when ready (hat, frame, mustache).

☐ Ask questions and have students respond to a virtual poll.

Use visuals and vocabulary strategies that support your objectives.

*T*eachers everywhere fill their "tool boxes" with as many strategies and instructional techniques as possible to help their students learn new material efficiently. Step 5 consists of specific tools that make a significant impact on instruction for all students, especially multilingual learners. Let's look at how using visuals and vocabulary strategies can help support our teaching objectives.

Use Visuals

Incorporating visuals in our lessons dramatically increases students' abilities to understand instructional content and discussions. It is said that "a picture is worth a thousand words," and often this is true. Photos, maps, drawings, movie clips, and concrete objects give students access to content despite possible barriers, such as lack of background on the subject or limited English (or target language) proficiency. For example, if the focus of the lesson (or the content objective [see p. 119]) is to explain safe lab procedures, showing photos of "safe" and "unsafe" activities will give students a stronger grasp of the core ideas.

Another effective visual tool is the graphic organizer. Graphic organizers provide a way for students to organize facts, ideas, and concepts that help them make sense of the content. You may already be familiar with a few of these. Teachers can use graphic organizers in every phase of a lesson:

» **Before instruction to provide a scaffold for new material and show how much students already know about a topic**

» **During instruction to help students organize key information**

» **After instruction to help students connect prior knowledge with new information and determine relationships between the two**

A variety of graphic organizers can effectively organize student thinking, including story maps, Venn diagrams, spider maps, T-charts, and KWL charts. When introducing a new type of graphic organizer, be sure to model its use and provide time for guided practice. As students become more skilled at using the organizers, they can create their own variations.

One strategy that promotes the use of visuals and takes very little planning in advance is Point and Talk. This strategy helps clarify the meanings of new concepts. Simply draw or show a visual of the key concept for each lesson. Keep it posted throughout the unit of study and consistently point back to it.

Let's use a language arts concept to illustrate this strategy. When teaching plot development, use a mountain visual like the one below. While discussing this vocabulary-dense concept, point to each stage to give students a visual anchor.

Climax

Rising Action

Falling Action

Exposition (Beginning)

Resolution (End)

Students who are learning another language need to receive comprehensible input (i.e., words and phrases they understand because of context clues). By consistently using Point and Talk throughout the lesson, teachers can actually increase how well their multilingual learners understand new content and provide an opportunity for them to acquire more of the target language.

Develop Vocabulary

It is important to incorporate content-specific terms in all of our lessons. A good rule of thumb is to introduce and display at least two new words per lesson. Here are two specific strategies that develop vocabulary comprehension.

HERE'S HOW IT WORKS

Scanning

Scanning is a powerful, quick, and efficient tool used to build academic language skills for students. This strategy teaches students essential words for understanding new content minutes before they encounter the words in a text. In fact, research has shown that student comprehension can increase by as much as 33 percent when teachers introduce specific key terms just before students read (Stahl & Fairbanks, 1986).

1. The students survey a text back to front (from the end to the beginning), looking for unfamiliar words.

2. The teacher generates a list of three to ten unfamiliar terms based on the students' survey.

3. The teacher writes short, student-friendly definitions for the terms, giving definitions that match the word's context in the passage.

4. The students practice pronouncing the words during a choral reading with the teacher.

5. The students read the passage.

6. The students use some of the words during speaking and writing tasks in the lesson. For example, students might include scanned words as they discuss the text with a partner or use them in a written summary.

Here's an example of how it might sound in a typical classroom:

Eighth Grade Science Dialogue
SCANNING

TEACHER *(Provides students with a handout containing word problems after modeling examples for the class.)* Okay, everyone, look at the handout, and let's do a quick scan of unfamiliar terms. Start at the bottom, scan toward the top, and circle two or more terms that you think you or someone else in the class cannot define. Put your pens down when you've finished circling. *(Students begin circling words on their handouts.)* Okay, I can see most of you have found a few words. *(Teacher pulls a name from his stack of index cards.)* Akeem, tell me one of the words you selected.

AKEEM Vehicle. *(Teacher pauses and glances at the poster that says, "Please express your thoughts in complete sentences.")* I selected the word vehicle, Mr. Eddie.

TEACHER *(Writes down "vehicle" on the dry-erase board.)* Thanks, Akeem. Patrice, what was one of the words you selected?

PATRICE I selected the word "uniform."

TEACHER *(Writes down the word "uniform" on the dry-erase board.)* Okay, does anyone else have a word we should include? Cleo?

CLEO I'm not sure what "velocity" is. I know we talked about it. Is that just like how fast something travels?

TEACHER Kind of. Let's write that down too. *(Writes "velocity.")* Anyone else? Okay. Can anyone think of a short definition for the word "vehicle"? Just call out an answer.

STUDENTS *(A few students speak out loud.)* A car, a truck. Something that moves you around.

TEACHER Let's write, "Something that carries you around, like a car or a truck." *(Teacher writes down the definition.)* Okay, what do you think "uniform" means in this sentence?

STUDENTS *(Calling out.)* Something you wear to school.

TEACHER Not quite. Not in this context. In this example from your book, "uniform" means something is the same rate the whole time. It's similar to the meaning of the word "constant." *(Teacher writes down the definition.)* Can someone tell me what "velocity" means?

DARRYL Does it mean the same thing as speed?

TEACHER Basically. It's the rate at which position changes. For now, let's write "speed" next to velocity.

TEACHER *(At the end of the class period.)* Okay, go ahead and fill out your science journals. Your sentence starter is on the board. Make sure you include at least one word from our scan: vehicle, uniform, or velocity.

When students read new written material, they often find unfamiliar vocabulary. To eliminate stumbling over new words, we can use scanning before reading a text in any content area. It doesn't take very much time for students to get used to this procedure, and it quickly builds an understanding of academic vocabulary. Scanning gives students some control over which vocabulary we emphasize, and it gives us the chance to focus on learning what students do not know instead of emphasizing what they already know.

HERE'S HOW IT WORKS

Marzano's Six-Step Vocabulary Process

Another approach for vocabulary development, outlined in Marzano's (2004) classic book Building Academic Vocabulary, is a comprehensive strategy for learning content-specific academic vocabulary, sometimes referred to as "brick words" (see p. 116), that students encounter in their reading. The first three steps help us introduce new terms; the last three steps help students practice and reinforce those terms over time. These steps are easily remembered as six D-words: Describe, Describe, Draw, Do, Discuss, Play.

Step 1, Describe: Instead of giving a formal definition of a vocabulary word or term, teachers give students a description or explanation of the word or term using examples and visuals. This could include sharing the meaning of prefixes, suffixes, and roots (morphological analysis) with students. The goal is to appeal to learners of all types in order to help them understand new vocabulary.

Step 2, Describe: Teachers ask students to describe or explain a vocabulary word or term using their own words. By listening to student descriptions/explanations, teachers can assess how well students have understood the meanings of the terms. Once teachers are sure all students have a basic understanding of the meaning of the terms, students then write descriptions of the terms in their personal notebooks to reference later.

Step 3, Draw: Teachers ask students to draw a representation of the new vocabulary word or term. Acceptable ways to complete this task include drawing pictures, designing symbols, making graphics, creating cartoons, and finding a visual online or in a magazine. These tasks can be done individually or in groups.

Step 4, Do: To give students more practice using new vocabulary words or terms, teachers have them participate in activities such as identifying prefixes, suffixes, synonyms, antonyms, related words, and additional visuals.

Step 5, Discuss: Teachers have students discuss the vocabulary words or terms as they work with partners, triads, or groups. This type of vocabulary discussion is more effective when it is structured (see p. 72). Additionally, monitoring student discussions can allow teachers to clarify any confusion students may have about the words or terms.

Step 6, Play: Students participate in games that reinforce a deep understanding of the new vocabulary words or terms. Examples of games include Jeopardy!®, Wordo (like bingo), Charades, Pictionary®, Scrabble®, etc.

Scanning and Marzano's Six-Step Vocabulary Process are two ways to teach vocabulary, but there are many other effective strategies we can use as long as they align with our lesson objectives and focus on helping students develop a deep understanding of academic vocabulary. For a more detailed discussion of writing effective lesson objectives (often referred to as content and language objectives), see pp. 118-123.

Another strategy that supports our lesson objectives is using sentence stems. This strategy helps students form complete sentences, and it allows them to grow accustomed to the kinds of words and phrases usually found in academic texts and conversations. Most importantly, however, sentence stems allow students to practice using new vocabulary words and terms in context. For example, when learning about the states of matter, the sentence stem, "One property of a solid is…" gives students a chance to practice using the words *property* and *solid* in the context of science.

The process of using a sentence stem begins when the teacher provides one as a starting point and instructs the students to use it in an oral or written response. At first, students will only use sentence stems when required to do so, but these supports will quickly become a part of classroom routines over time.

There are two types of sentence stems: general and specific. A general stem can be used in any content area to figure out what our students are thinking and to determine the amount of background knowledge a student has on any given topic. Examples of general stems include, "I learned…," "I already know…," and, "I agree/disagree with _____ because…"

Unlike general stems, specific sentence stems are tied to a particular content area or lesson. We use specific stems to check for understanding of the learning objectives. Examples of specific stems are, "One cause of the Civil War was…," "Photosynthesis is…," and, "I think _____ is the protagonist because…" Using general and specific sentence stems gives students many risk-free opportunities to speak and write using academic language.

General Stem	Specific Stem
I learned...	I learned that a new way to calculate amortization is...
I already know...	I already know that authors use characterization to...
I agree/disagree with ____ because...	I agree/disagree with the idea that Byron should spend the summer with his grandma in Birmingham because...

"Step 5 - Use visual and vocabulary strategies that support your objectives. Students can better conceptualize new vocabulary when they see models to associate with new words, especially with ELs, SpEd, and any heterogenous classes."

ESL Teacher, Frisco ISD

We find it helpful to look at our assessments as guides to developing sentence stems for students to use. Both standardized assessments and local assessments often have sentence structures and terminology that are unfamiliar to students. Creating sentence stems based on some of the assessment questions gives students a chance to practice using academic language.

Sentence stems provide a framework for students to gradually use increasing amounts of academic language. When our students have opportunities to practice using the words and phrases they will encounter on an assessment, they are better prepared for those assessments because the language used will be familiar to them. By strategically using general and specific sentence stems, we change the way students talk. When we change the way they talk, we open the door to new ways of thinking.

Examples:

Test Question	Sentence Stem
Which word from paragraph 2 means the same thing as "sinister"?	*The word from the paragraph that means the same thing as sinister is…*
What speed record did Alma exceed by exactly 4.66 miles per hour?	*The record Alma exceeded by exactly 4.66 miles per hour was…*
How did the invention of the printing press affect the flow of ideas in Europe in the 1500s?	*The invention of the printing press affected the flow of ideas in Europe in the 1500s by…*

WHAT RESEARCH SAYS

Students with learning barriers often have difficulty recalling newly learned content, so connecting concepts with detailed visuals can support vocabulary comprehension in all content areas. Fountas and Pinnell (2001) stated that when content is illustrated with diagrams, students will be better equipped to maintain the information over time and apply the knowledge in multiple contexts. Research has shown that the use of graphic organizers can help students take charge of their learning processes and that these visual instructional elements support student understanding and achievement across all content areas (Uba et al., 2017). Maccini and Gagnon (2000) also found that using graphic organizers in math class may lessen students' difficulties with math concepts. The specific ways we support multilingual learners through visual vocabulary strategies create the necessary scaffolding for language acquisition.

Vocabulary strategies that aid in long-term content retention and application require teachers to utilize metacognitive strategies that prompt active student involvement in learning the words. To develop metacognitive strategies, teachers must plan, monitor, and evaluate learning experiences while students attempt to acquire vocabulary (Chamot & O'Malley, 1996). This could include strategies such as morphological analysis, which has shown significant benefits for lower-performing students such as ELs and students with reading disabilities (Brandes & McMaster, 2017). Using vocabulary strategies and sentence stems has also been shown to improve student achievement for English learners (Echevarria et al., 2017; Wessell, 2011). In addition to these strategies, pre-teaching terms enhances student reading comprehension in both synchronous and asynchronous learning environments. In fact, Stahl and Fairbanks (1986) demonstrated that student comprehension soars when specific key terms are introduced prior to reading and learning.

Step it UP!

Good teachers instinctively use visual aids and vocabulary strategies to create effective lessons. But how does this look different in a 7 Steps classroom? The question we need to ask is, "Will these visuals and vocabulary strategies help students be able to use content-specific words associated with higher levels of thinking?"

To STEP IT UP, we need to empower students to communicate effectively using complex, content-specific language. Not only do students need to know this vocabulary, but they must be able to apply, analyze, evaluate, and create using the new words they learn. The chart below lists different kinds of common vocabulary strategies at different levels of Bloom's taxonomy.

Remember	Flash cards, matching
Understand	Writing personal descriptions of word meanings
Apply	Using vocabulary words in sentences
Analyze	Sorting and categorizing vocabulary words
Evaluate	Judging levels of understanding, critiquing the use of words
Create	Drawing images, creating diagrams to show understanding

Frequently Asked Questions

1 What types of visual and vocabulary strategies can I use to encourage students to think at higher levels?

We encourage higher levels of thinking when we help students develop robust, content-specific use of vocabulary and visuals. One tool for doing this effectively is the use of **Interactive Word Walls.** These allow students to process vocabulary and concepts they are learning at a deeper level. Having these available in both physical and online formats creates resources for all learning environments. Structured in the form of a graphic organizer with visuals, graphics, and even realia, Interactive Word Walls allow students to literally see relationships among the terms.

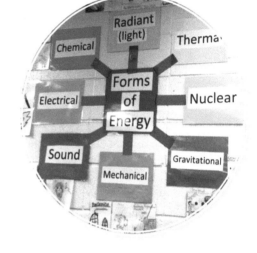

Giving students ownership in creating the word wall requires them to analyze and evaluate vocabulary words to create an organizer that accurately and creatively displays the relationships between the terms. Since Interactive Word Walls can be thematic and changed with each unit, students will have multiple opportunities to apply in-depth thinking about the words and concepts they are learning.

Allowing students to update and maintain these interactive resources also increases the amount of time students can use them to support content language development.

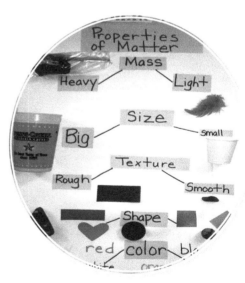

WATCH
Develop Academic
Language with
Word Walls

In addition to word walls, the following activities can also be used to enhance vocabulary instruction and move students to higher levels of thinking:

Activity	Description
Card Sort	Students are given a set of cards with pictures and/or words and asked to sort them into categories. Sample categories could include living vs. nonliving, states of matter, types of energy, etc. While students are sorting the cards, they ask their group members questions like the following: *What does this picture show?* *What category would be good for this card?* *How can we be sure these cards all go together?* *Which rule are we using to categorize this card?*
Choose the Words	Students select words from a word wall or word list to use in a conversation or writing.
Idea Frames	Sentence frames like the ones below help students organize schema for new words (Marzano et al., 2001; Hill & Flynn, 2006). *Compare: __ is similar to __ in that both...* *Contrast: __ is different from __ in that...* *Analogy: __ is to __ as __ is to __.* *Metaphor: I think ____ is...* *Simile: I think __ is like/as...because...*
Concept Definition Map	This visual organizer enables students to process a term using four questions (Echevarria, et al., 2017). *What is the term?* *What is it?* *What is it like?* *What are some examples?*
Creating Words	This vocabulary game provides an opportunity for students to review key vocabulary by using words in creative ways. To start, a student selects a word and rolls a cube with the following on its sides: model it, draw it, act it out, write about it, talk about it, rap about it, etc. Based on the outcome of the roll, the student represents the word and the classmates guess it.
Graffiti Write	In small groups, students simultaneously list academic words tied to a particular concept within a short time frame.
List, Group, Label	Students are given a list of content-specific vocabulary words. They sort the words on this list into similar piles and create labels for each pile. This can be done by topic (planets, stars, scientific laws, etc.) or by word type (those beginning with a particular letter, those with a specific suffix, or those in a certain tense) (Taba, 1967).

Activity	Description
Personal Dictionary	Students choose words from the word wall, wordlists, or words encountered in texts. Words are recorded on note cards or in notebooks that become personal dictionaries. Students are encouraged to draw, reflect, or use their native language when writing definitions (Adapted from Echevarria et al., 2017).
Say it Another Way Chart (Dead Word Cemetery)	This strategy enriches student vocabulary and increases the ability to describe phenomena and people using academic language. For this activity, teachers provide sophisticated alternatives for high-frequency words and then give students multiple opportunities to use those alternatives. Using the "Say it Another Way Chart" or "Dead Word Cemetery" helps students apply academic language they may not use in ordinary descriptions. It also allows students to be playful and have fun while engaging in academic conversation with low-frequency academic vocabulary.
Vocabulary Game Shows	Using games like Jeopardy!®, Pictionary®, and Who Wants to Be a Millionaire?®, etc., allows students a chance to practice academic vocabulary.
Word Play	In this activity, students manipulate words through various word games designed to increase understanding. Johnson et al. (2004) divide word games into eight categories: onomastics (name games), expressions, figures of speech, word associations, word formations, word manipulations, word games, and ambiguities.
Word Splash	Select key vocabulary words or words connected to a concept and write them for students to see. Tell students you wrote the words in no particular order (called a splash). Have students begin to categorize the words in some logical order. Ask students to choose the words from one category to use in a written paragraph, and then ask them to share their paragraphs orally with the class.

 Should we have students look up the words that have been scanned in a dictionary and write the definitions down?

No. This will take too much time. Scanning is a quick process. Our goal is to give students the meaning of the scanned words within the context of their reading for that specific lesson. Having students look up isolated words in the dictionary does not meet this goal because they will encounter multiple definitions riddled with more unfamiliar words.

3 Why does the scan process seem backward, going from the end to the beginning of a passage?

Scanning from end to beginning helps the student focus on unfamiliar words and terms without reading the text. The unfamiliar words and terms will be more identifiable while scanning backward because students will not focus on comprehending the full text. By keeping the focus solely on identifying unfamiliar vocabulary, the scan procedure moves along quickly.

4 The vocabulary techniques (Scanning and the Six-Step Vocabulary Process) are nice ideas, but will they take too much time?

They do take time, but these techniques are well worth the investment because they increase student comprehension and understanding.

When students scan for unfamiliar words before reading a text, they will be more confident and successful during the reading task. When working with content-specific vocabulary in multiple ways, students gain a deeper understanding of the words and internalize the meanings of those words.

5 Is there more we can do with vocabulary words so students will really learn them?

Yes. One great idea is to post them on an Interactive Word Wall in the classroom. A word wall is a place for lists of words that change over time. On the word wall, we can list scan words from written material, key content concepts, or words that might be helpful for students to use in writing or conversation. Some teachers put short definitions next to the words, and others don't. The most important thing about the words we post is to ensure that students have multiple opportunities to use the words when they write and speak.

Here are some other ideas:

1. Offer incentives or positive feedback for using the words/terms.

2. Require the use of specific words/terms in a warm-up writing assignment or in a learning journal at the end of class.

3. Specify that a certain number of words/terms be used in written assignments during class for reviews, essays, or notes.

4. Encourage the use of specific words/terms in whole-class or student-to-student conversation.

6 Should we give students a sentence stem for every key concept?

It's a good idea. Using sentence stems is perfect for introducing concepts and for assessing student understanding during a lesson. They provide the academic language students need to communicate using new and unusual terms. When sentence stems are used consistently in the classroom, students automatically start to respond in complete sentences without reminders. The habit of reframing the language of the question into a response is a skill that students internalize through multiple practice opportunities as well as teacher modeling.

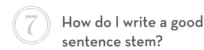

**How do I write a good
sentence stem?**

The easiest way to create meaningful sentence stems is to start with the learning
objectives for each lesson. What should students be able to do at the end of the
lesson? Think of one question for students to answer that shows mastery of the
material. Next, use the academic language in the question to create a sentence
stem. For example, one of the first learning objectives in many science classes is for
students to know safe lab procedures. A question to ask students might be, "What
are three safety procedures to use during a lab?" Using the academic language from
the question, an appropriate sentence stem would be, "Three safety procedures to
use during a lab are…"

Not all stems are focused on a specific content area like the previous example. The
generic sentence stems listed below can be used in any classroom or subject area.

Purpose	Stem
Summarizing	I learned… Today I realized… I still wonder… The most significant thing I learned today was… I would summarize my learning by saying… My initial thought was __, and now I'm thinking __ because…
Sharing	I feel… In my opinion… I predict that… I agree/disagree that… My view on the matter is __ because…
Justifying	I think __ because… I agree/disagree with __ because… __ proves that… Another idea might be __ because… I was thinking that __ should be… __ corroborates the idea that…
Accessing Prior Knowledge	I already know… __ reminds me of… My experience with… I would like to know more about… I would compare __ to __ because… Discussing __ made me consider…
Elaborating	__ is important because… I chose __ because… The answer might also be __ because… I would agree or disagree with __ because… Another reason could be… I would add __ because…

How does Step 5 promote language acquisition for MLLs?

Students need to associate what they are learning with more than just vocabulary. Seidlitz & Perryman (2011) stated, "When working with content-specific vocabulary in multiple ways, students gain a deeper understanding of the words, and they internalize their meanings" (p. 40). This is especially true for English learners who may have obstacles to understanding text, so it is important to incorporate other ways to help students make sense of what they are learning. The use of nonlinguistic representations (Hill & Miller, 2013) is an excellent way to further engage students who are challenged by content vocabulary. There are five suggested categories teachers can use to associate what is being learned with another form of content processing:

» Engage students in kinesthetic activities
» Use graphic organizers
» Make physical models or use manipulatives
» Generate mental pictures
» Create pictures, illustrations, or pictographs

WATCH
Visuals and Vocabulary in the Science Classroom

NOTES FROM THE FIELD

"I have seen teachers share their own images, drawings, and texts using the document camera or iPad. I have also seen teachers effectively draw students' attention to vocabulary, specific letters/words, and editing marks using the mouse."

- Mónica Lara

"A teacher at a recent training shared that she used 'treasure boxes' (any box the kids found around the house, such as baby wipes boxes, cereal boxes, shoeboxes, etc.) with her kindergarten students. When they came to a word they did not know, students would write the word and draw a picture to add to their treasure box. As students learned words, they could remove the ones that were no longer 'treasures' as they became part of their vocabularies."

- Allison Hand

The virtual classroom offers many unique opportunities for effectively using visual and vocabulary strategies that support your objectives. In some ways, using visuals is actually easier in a virtual environment than in face-to-face instruction.

For example, we can easily use the mouse to track text and refer to visuals while reading aloud or explaining concepts. There are a variety of platforms that allow teachers to create truly interactive word walls. In addition, there are also many online "games" we can use to reinforce the learning of new vocabulary.

Introducing objectives is another great opportunity to use visuals to reinforce language acquisition during virtual instruction. We can color-code keywords in our objectives and visually annotate them to make them more comprehensible. We can also use the chat to have students paraphrase their own understandings of both the lesson objectives and key ideas throughout the lesson.

Content Objective:
We will identify the seven steps to a language-rich, interactive **classroom by discussing and practicing each step.**

Can you say this using other words?

Type your way to this objective in

Content Objective:
We will identify the seven steps to a language-rich, interactive **classroom by discussing and practicing each step.**

Language Objective:
We will write a reflection using: "One challenge English learners face is…"

Seidlitz

☐ Tracking text with the mouse

☐ Easily accessible images for teachers/students to pair with vocabulary

☐ Online platforms conducive to Interactive Word Walls

☐ Visually annotating objectives on screen (with simplified synonyms)

☐ Students paraphrasing their comprehension in the chat (putting key vocabulary in their own words)

Step 6

Have students participate **in structured conversations.**

Asking students to talk with each other using specific language about a clearly defined topic is called structured conversation. Structured conversations allow students a chance to share ideas and points of view with each other.

When we are explicit about how students are to engage in discussion, it reduces a lot of the problems that arise when we ask them to work together in groups. During structured conversations, we often see an enhanced understanding of topics, less off-task behavior, and fewer classroom management problems.

So how exactly does a structured conversation happen? A structured conversation occurs whenever we have a small group of students use sentence frames to engage in a short conversation about a topic. The teacher monitors the conversation to ensure all students can participate fully. Before setting up the structured conversation, it is important to make sure that students have enough background information and an adequate grasp of the content to be discussed. In doing this, teachers can make structured conversations a particularly effective piece of classroom instruction.

Although using the structured conversation format is a proven way to facilitate the use of complex, content-specific language in the classroom, sometimes we avoid the strategy because we think it will take away valuable instructional time. On the contrary, structured conversations can be as short as thirty-five seconds or (if a topic really engages the students) as long as five minutes. A simple strategy that weaves structured conversation into instruction is **QSSSA** (Question, Signal, Stem, Share, Assess). This chapter will focus on this particular structure because it is the simplest way to include all the necessary elements of

HERE'S HOW IT WORKS

Question

Signal

Stem

Share

Assess

EXAMPLE

1. **Question** — Ask a question pertaining to the content.
2. **Signal** — Provide a way to indicate readiness.
3. **Stem** — Provide students with a sentence stem to respond to the question. Wait for all students to show the signal.
4. **Share** — Beginning with a given sentence stem, students share their responses with a peer.
5. **Assess** — The teacher randomly assesses students by calling on them individually.

an effective structured conversation. In a QSSSA, the teacher asks a question, and the students give a response signal when they are ready to answer. Using a sentence stem, students share their responses with one or more peers. Finally, the teacher assesses the quality of the discussion by randomly selecting a few students to share their answers with the whole class. Students could also share by writing and then reading their responses.

We want to model the process the first few times and ensure that students know which sentence stems and academic vocabulary to use in the exercise. In fact, consistently using sentence stems in structured conversations is always an opportunity to increase in-context exposure to content-specific vocabulary.

QSSSA Step *Purpose for the step*	Sounds Like:
Question *Check Understanding*	Ok I don't want anyone to shout out. I just want everyone to think about this: _____ *(Silently count to 3.)*
Signal *Processing Time*	When you've got an idea or know the answer, show me by: _____ *(Wait for majority of students to show the signal. Repeat question if needed.)*
Stem *Target Academic Language*	Here is how I'd like for you to share: _____ Let's all practice this stem together. *(Make sure the stem is displayed/posted.)*
Share *100% of Students Practice Academic Language*	Now I'm going to let you share with your partner. _____, you'll go first. _____, you'll share second.
Assess *Accountability and Check Understanding*	Ok, let's come back together. I'd like to hear some of your great ideas. I'm going to _____. If you get called on, you can share your idea or your partner's. Be sure to use our stem.

Elementary Structured Conversation Example:

Question	Signal	Stem	Share	Assess
Math What is the sum of three and four?	Raise hand when ready to respond →	The sum of three and four is...	Turn to Your Partner, Random Calling on Students	Students solve problems 1-5 in workbook
Social Studies Do you agree/ disagree with Rosa Parks' decision to...?	Thinker's Chin →	I agree/ disagree with Rosa Parks' decision because...	Numbered Heads Together	Explain or illustrate, in journals, one thing you would have done
Science What is a characteristic of an insect?	Stand when ready →	One charac-teristic of an insect is...	Think, Pair, Share	Label or illustrate some characteris-tics of insects
Language Arts What is the main idea?	Put your pen down when finished writing a response →	The main idea is...	Inside/Outside Circle	Randomize and ro-tate responses with whole group

Here are some examples of QSSSA in the content area classrooms:

	Question	Signal	Stem	Share	Assess
Math	What are some important things to remember when deriving the equation of a parabola?	Raise your hand when you can complete this sentence →	One important thing to remember when deriving the equation of a parabola is... because...	Share in groups of three	Randomly call on students
Social Studies	Do you support Sam Houston's position on secession?	Place your hand on your chin when you can complete this sentence →	I support/ oppose Sam Houston's position because...	Numbered Heads Together	Randomly select groups to respond
Science	What are some unusual characteristics of annelids?	Stand up when you can complete this sentence →	The most unusual characteristic of annelids is... because...	Share in groups of two	Randomly call on students
Language Arts	Do you think Esperanza's family made a wise decision?	Put your pen down when you can complete this sentence →	I think Esperanza's family made/did not make a wise decision because...	Share answers with several partners	Have students write their perspectives in journals

Here's how a structured conversation might sound in a typical classroom:

Ninth Grade Algebra Dialogue
QSSSA

TEACHER What is the first step you would take to factor this equation? Please stand when you can finish this sentence: "The first step I would take to factor this equation is..." *(Teacher waits until all students stand before proceeding.)* Using the sentence stem given, turn to the person standing nearest to you and tell them your answer. If you agree with your partner, say, "I agree because..." If you don't agree, say, "I disagree because..." Okay, ready, go.

STUDENTS The first step I would take in factoring this equation is... *(Teacher waits until all students finish sharing before proceeding.)*

TEACHER Okay, what is the first step you would take to factor this equation? *(Teacher randomly selects a name from a stack of cards.)* Alex?

ALEX The first step I would take in factoring this equation would be to put like terms together.

TEACHER Tell me more about that.

11th Grade Physics Dialogue
QSSSA

TEACHER What are some characteristics of waves? Please raise your hand when you can finish this sentence, "Some characteristics of waves are..." *(Students all raise their hands.)* Turn to the person next to you and say your whole sentence. If you agree with the person, say, "I agree because..." If you disagree, say, "I disagree because..." Now, turn to each other and begin sharing.

TEACHER Okay, what is one characteristic of a wave? *(Teacher randomly selects a name from a stack of cards.)* Malia?

MALIA One characteristic of a wave is that it has a specific amplitude.

TEACHER Thank you, Malia.

WATCH
QSSSA
in Action

Try This! Another Strategy for Structured Conversations
W.I.T. Questioning

To expand student conversation as well as to promote elaboration, teachers can encourage the use of these W.I.T. Questioning stems to keep the discussion going:

Why do you think...?

Is there another...?

Tell me more about...

WHAT RESEARCH SAYS

When students use structured conversations to explore content-area objectives, and defend opinions, their emotions are engaged in an energizing and meaningful way. Small-group conversations with clear instructional goals allow student discussions to develop around the topic to be governed by the students' input rather than teacher direction. Marzano et al. (2001) stated that when students are asked to defend different perspectives, many new ideas are generated and concepts are understood at a deeper level. Student voices evolve as they share critical and insightful points of view and experience empathy listening to others' thoughts and worldviews, both of which are significant factors in deeply understanding academic concepts (Wiggins & McTighe, 1998). Chadha (2019) highlighted the use of peer interaction for content-area conversations in the virtual learning environment to boost academic progression and engage students in deeper learning, stating that it is "imperative that instructors design online spaces for students to interact with each other...giving them time to think critically and build relationships" (p. 36).

Short (2017) stated that using techniques such as sentence stems in structured conversations can guide student output for greater understanding. As a critical component to increasing student engagement, The 7 Steps Study (Goldman et al., 2021) identified the importance of this particular collaborative structure in enhancing oracy and developing language skills for students at the beginning and intermediate levels of English proficiency.

Student-to-student interaction focused on lesson concepts has been shown to have significant effects on student achievement (Marzano et al., 2001). This may be because structured conversations ensure that students gain exposure to content-specific vocabulary as well as a chance to use new terms in an authentic context. In several studies, students who participated in structured conversations about a topic showed greater speaking proficiency than students who did not. The use of oral discourse in mathematics classes has also been shown to increase proficiency when students talk and write about their thinking (Gearing & Hart, 2019). Some types of learning actually require focused student-to-student conversation. Levine (2019) found that high school students need help constructing interpretations of literature—which only happens through repeated conversations in which students have the opportunity to elaborate on the meaning of texts.

Step it UP!

To write open-ended questions, try starting the question with "why," "how," or "what if." Once we have established a classroom culture where all students regularly participate in conversations using complex, content area language, we are ready to go deeper. We can now have students engage in extended structured conversations, but this time from multiple points of view. Taking on a variety of perspectives allows students to reach higher levels of thinking and creates a positive classroom culture by building empathy for different viewpoints. This also helps students develop crucial skills necessary for argumentative literacy (the ability to make and understand reasoned arguments) and engage in meaningful discussions as they use complex language to defend their ideas.

When planning lessons, we can gradually move students toward more complex thinking, helping them learn to think critically from multiple perspectives by carefully structuring our questions and the sequence of our lessons. The chart below shows examples of how we can help students shift from giving only fact-based answers to speaking from multiple perspectives:

Perspective	Description	Language Arts Example	Science Example
Giving a fact-based answer	All students and the teacher have the same answer.	What issues related to technology are addressed in the novel Frankenstein?	Why are some communities having trouble accessing fresh water?
Citing a point of view	Students cite someone else's perspective on an issue.	What were Mary Shelly's fears about technology?	What does the author of the article think is a good way to address the water conservation crisis?
Giving a personal point of view	Students share their perspectives on an issue.	Do you think there are examples of modern technology "going too far"?	What do you think is the best way to deal with the water conservation crisis in the western United States?
Speaking from multiple perspectives	Students are able to defend multiple perspectives on an issue.	Why do people disagree about ethical issues related to genetic engineering? How would both sides intelligently defend their point of view?	Why do people disagree about how to address the water conservation crisis? How would scientists who differ on this issue defend their ideas?

Frequently Asked Questions

 How do I develop structured conversations that encourage students to use higher-level thinking and multiple perspectives?

If students are already comfortable knowing what to say instead of "I don't know," speaking in complete sentences, using response signals, and using sentence stems in short, structured conversations, they will be better able to participate and stay focused during extended interactions from different perspectives.

Wiggins and McTighe (1998) define perspective as having "critical and insightful points of view" and empathy as "the ability to get inside another person's feelings and worldview." By asking students to defend different perspectives, we can encourage them to generate many new ideas and understand
concepts at a deeper level. When students use structured conversations to defend a perspective, their emotions are engaged in an energized and meaningful way. Emotions underlie the processes that create memory, meaning, and attention.

Moreover, conversations from multiple perspectives require students to use higher-level thinking skills that deepen their understanding of the concept they are studying. Structured conversations such as the ones below can become an integral part of everyday instruction. Here are three examples:

Expert/Novice

This activity is especially suited for science and math classes because students often become confused about the processes involved in various steps/ procedures in these subjects.

WATCH

Here are the steps:

1. Students brainstorm questions a novice might ask about a procedure or process.

2. Students list possible answers an expert might give to the questions.

3. Students form pairs (A, B). One student plays the role of a novice, and the other student is the expert.

4. The teacher asks a few students to model their conversations in front of the class.

The Expert/Novice activity becomes more engaging if students can take on different roles during the activity. They can be scientists at NASA talking to tourists or math tutors from a university talking to freshmen struggling with basic concepts. For some students, playing a formal role helps them feel less inhibited. At times, we have seen the model conversations that follow this activity involve humor and style. This makes the activity memorable to the students, and these conversations help build a sense of community in the classroom.

T-Chart, Pair, Defend

This structured conversation allows students to approach a content concept from two opposing viewpoints.

1. Choose a text that will enable students to have a vocabulary-rich conversation from two different points of view.

2. Select a pair of characters related to the text who could have two different points of view. Characters could be from a novel or short story, scientists making a decision, or lawmakers debating a bill.

3. Have students read and annotate the text.

4. Have students brainstorm possible attitudes and beliefs of the two selected characters from the text on a T-chart.

5. Have students form pairs and take turns role-playing conversations. The conversation always begins with a structured sentence frame.

WATCH
Foster Interactions
with T-Chart,
Pair, Defend

Here are some examples of possible topics and sentence starters:

Subject	Topic	Sentence Starters	
		A	B
Social Studies	Crusades	We should leave England for the Holy Land because…	We should stay in England because…
Science	The Use of Ethanol for Energy	We must convert America to an ethanol-based economy because…	We should not convert America to an ethanol-based economy because…
Language Arts	The Three Little Pigs	The wolf should blow all the houses down because…	The wolf should not blow all the houses down because…
Math	Setting Up Word Problems	We should set up a table and make a sketch before setting up these equations because…	We should not set up a table and make a sketch before setting up these equations because…
Art	Drawing with Perspective	It's easy to draw with perspective because…	It's difficult to draw with perspective because…

Perspective Choice

After reading and discussing a topic, students are assigned points of view and given stems that help them engage in discussion from a particular perspective. For example, four to six scientists with different perspectives on how to address climate change or four to six civil rights activists discussing the Montgomery bus boycott.

Here are the steps:

After reading and discussing a topic in science or social studies, select a situation in which a group of six people must make a decision. Examples include a family of medieval peasants deciding whether or not to go on a pilgrimage or a group of scientists trying to determine how to handle an epidemic.

As a class, write six different sentences representing different perspectives on the same event using the sentence frames such as these:

Sentence Stems

I think we should __ because...
We ought to __ because...
It would be a good idea to...
We definitely shouldn't __ because...
It's not wise to __ because...
I don't believe it is worthwhile to __ because...

For example:

1. "I think we should go on the pilgrimage because we've never been before."

2. "We ought to go because we will be able to visit some of the fairs and trade our goods."

3. "It would be a good idea to go because St. James' prayers are known to be helpful."

4. "We definitely shouldn't go because I've heard towns in that area may have the plague."

5. "It's not wise to go because there are too many thieves along the road."

6. "I don't believe it's worthwhile to go because we have too much work to do here on the farm."

Number the perspectives one through six and have students form small groups of six, each student taking a different perspective. Students begin by reading a sentence from the board and then improvising a conversation based on their impression of what the characters might say. Students may repeat their conversations as a class. The class as a whole then discusses what might be the best choice for the group.

"Students participate in structured conversations because this (1) seems to help teachers incorporate academic, standard-based vocabulary with students and (2) it encourages ALL students to talk during lessons."
Dr. Jennifer Valdez
Deputy Superintendent of Academics
Alvin ISD

② Why should I use structured conversations and not simply call on students randomly in the classroom, one student at a time?

First, structured conversations are much more engaging because the process includes 100 percent student participation. In single-student questioning, the teacher selects one student at a time to respond to a question while everyone else in the classroom remains passive. With structured conversations, every student remains active throughout the activity: crafting responses to the question by completing the sentence stem, demonstrating completion and readiness with the chosen response signal, sharing their responses with partners or in groups, and finally being held accountable for their responses in the assessment. This process provides enough structure to get all students involved both physically and mentally. It maximizes engagement time in the classroom and minimizes single-student responses. Introducing your students to structured conversations such as QSSSA early in the school year and training them to use these strategies will get everyone accustomed to the process quickly.

③ Do we have the time to have structured conversations in the classroom?

First, let's stop and think about what we are currently doing with our students during the class period. Is it effective? What percentage of time during each class are our students engaged in learning? What percentage of the time are our students thinking critically? How often do our students get the chance to verbalize and internalize the content they're studying? Are students in our classrooms actively involved, or are they sitting passively?

Activities that structure student conversationfrom different points of view provide the framework for total student engagement and foster a sense of understanding of the content, both cognitively and critically. This is quality education.

Structured conversations such as QSSSA take minimal preparation and are simple to implement. Considering what is expected of our students regarding accountability and academic growth, do we have time not to implement Step 6?

"Structured conversations have had a profound impact on instruction in our district. One of our favorites is QSSSA because it is a great way to engage ALL learners. We attribute much of our TELPAS (language assessment) growth to the implementation of structured conversations. When we can get every student talking, we can get every student learning!"

Sara Sparks
ESL Specialist
Hays CISD

4 I like the idea of structured conversations, but I'm afraid my students might not want to participate in them.

Some students may initially resist some of the procedures of an interactive classroom and multiple-perspective activities. Remember, we are nudging them out of their passive comfort zones into a new learning zone. However, if structured conversation is implemented properly in a well-managed environment, students will quickly become successful with the new procedures and understand them as a fun and successful way to learn.

On the first day of school, we should begin to nourish a climate of trust and accountability. When Step 6 is introduced and carefully developed, students will become accustomed to engaging in an interactive, language-rich classroom.

WATCH
Inside/Outside
Circles for
Reluctant Students

5 What happens if students will not participate in the structured conversations?

Initially, there may be reluctance or hesitation by some students. Keep in mind that we are nudging our students from a very well-learned pattern of passivity into something that is much more engaging. Once students understand and experience success with the process, they usually enjoy it and look forward to participating in it.

For students who need extra encouragement, we simply provide the sentence stem in advance for them to practice. If need be, we can actually give them a phrase or answer to complete the given sentence stem. Initially, we may have to push and support the students as they become accustomed to structured conversations. With encouragement, support, and repetition, even our most reluctant students will soon feel comfortable and will join the process.

6   I don't understand the "A" of QSSSA.

The "A" of QSSSA stands for assess. This kind of assessment pertains to feedback and not grading (i.e., formative, not summative assessment). The process is simple. After students have shared their completed sentence stems with a peer, the teacher can assess their responses by randomly calling on individual students. Students can share their sentence stems or write about their learning experiences during the structured conversation, as well. These sharing strategies allow the teacher to assess responses and check student understanding. Teachers are not evaluating students; instead, they use student responses to know whether to reteach or move forward with the lesson. Other assessment methods include whole-class written responses or the Numbered Heads Together strategy (see p. 38) with teams of students reporting their responses to the rest of the class.

> "Structured conversations have raised student engagement and content mastery. Students are exposed multiple times to academic language and concepts through strategies like QSSSA, and everyone has a chance to give and receive answers. We use this strategy in a multitude of ways, and it is always my go-to as it hits several steps in and of itself. Students who were hesitant to respond because they didn't know the answer or because of limited English are given opportunities to participate and share in a strategy like QSSSA."
>
> Ashley Gomez
> District EL Specialist
> Alvin ISD

NOTES FROM THE FIELD

"Have younger students bring a fuzzy friend (stuffed animal) to class. When it is time to practice speaking, prompt the students to 'whisper their answer to their fuzzy friend.' Teachers can see which students are speaking and encourage those who are not. 100 percent choral response allows all students to practice the vocabulary."

- Allison Hand

How do I implement Step 6 in a virtual environment?

Virtual classrooms present many options for having students participate in structured conversations. Each part of QSSSA (Question, Signal, Stem, Share, Assess) can be effectively implemented when teaching virtually. The examples below walk through various approaches.

☐ Have students share in breakout rooms, on a shared document, or by responding to each other in the chat.

☐ For assessing student conversations, have students report on what other students in their group said or typed.

☐ For younger students who do not use breakout rooms, follow the QSSSA format except during the "share," when you can have them whisper to their "fuzzy friend."

☐ During an asynchronous QSSSA, use an online tool that allows students to post responses at various times.

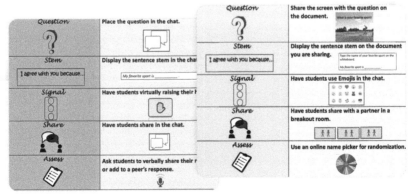

Images of QSSSA in the virtual classroom provided by Joël Johnson, Secondary ESL Coordinator

Have students participate in **structured reading and writing activities.**

The goal of Step 7 is to structure reading and writing activities so students gain a deep understanding of content concepts while developing complex, content-specific language. Although students read and write frequently in our classes, they benefit when we create structure by clearly defining our purpose, plan, and process for each reading or writing activity.

Structured Reading Activities

All reading activities should have a clear purpose. In other words, we should be able to answer this question: "Why am I having my students read this?" We select a text that students will read based on the content objectives for the lesson. We also align the reading activities with the language objectives to give us a clear focus on how we will use language during the task.

Once the purpose for the reading activity is defined, we need to make a plan. Asking, "How will I make sure my students are ready to read this?" helps the planning process. We need to decide whether students are ready to read the text independently, and if they are not, we need to put supports in place to ensure their success. To prepare students to read independently, we can establish prior knowledge of the reading task, scan the text for unfamiliar words, and allow students to partner read.

SCAFFOLDS TO SUPPORT READING

» Annotated/accommodated text

» Targeted translation

» Visual supports

» Opportunities to partner read

» Scanning before reading

» Previewing new vocabulary and concepts

When students engage in a reading task, we want to think about what strategies they will use to make sense of the text. Different types of texts require different strategies. For example, the thinking that goes on while reading a fairy tale is very different from the thinking required when reading a word problem in math class.

"By being intentional in our planning, Step 7 (Structured Reading and Writing Activities) has really helped a lot of educators reframe their literacy instruction through a language lens. While maintaining high expectations for all, we can provide supports and scaffolds to support students in reading and writing across content areas."

Carly Spina
District EL Bilingual Instructional Coach

Here are two specific strategies that help students understand various texts:

Somebody-Wanted-But-So

The Somebody-Wanted-But-So strategy (Macon et al., 1991), used during or after reading, helps students understand literary elements such as conflicts and resolutions. It is also an excellent summarization technique for social studies since so much of world history is based on the wants and needs of humans. Students determine the main character (somebody), his/her motivation (wanted), the main conflict (but), and the resolution to the conflict (so).

Somebody	Wanted	But	So
The Big Bad Wolf	Pigs for dinner	They hid in the brick house.	He tried to go down the chimney to get them.
The African American citizens of Montgomery, AL	The buses to be desegregated	The white business owners refused to desegregate.	The citizens launched a boycott against the buses.

Summarization Frames

Students sometimes struggle with making sense of nonfiction text in content-area classes, and providing specific strategies for organizing and summarizing can often help. Each content area may require a different approach for students to organize their thinking about a given text. The chart below provides specific stems and questions that help students summarize the text in math, science, and social studies.

Math	Science	Social Studies
The problem says...	The main idea(s) in this explanation/passage are...	The main idea(s) in this explanation/passage are...
The problem is asking me to...	Some important words in this explanation/passage are...	Some important words in this explanation/passage are...
The table/picture/graph shows...	What does the word __ mean?	What does the word __ mean?
Some important words in this problem/explanation are...	I think the word __ means...	I think the word __ means...
What does the word __ mean?	The table/picture/graph shows...	The table/picture/graph shows...
I think the word __ means...	Based on the information found in __, I can conclude/infer...	Who? Did what? Where? When? Why?
The steps to solve this are...		

Other examples of Structured Reading Activities:

Reading Activity	Description
SQP2RS ("Squeepers")	A classroom reading strategy that trains students to use cognitive and metacognitive strategies to process nonfiction text. The steps are Survey, Question, Predict, Read, Respond, and Summarize (Echevarria et al., 2017).
Cornell Notes	A method of note-taking in which paper is divided into two columns. In one large column, students take traditional notes in outline form. In the second column, students write key vocabulary terms and questions (Pauk & Owens, 2013).
Idea Bookmarks	Students take reflective notes on bookmark-sized pieces of paper. The bookmarks include questions, observations, and words from the reading that strike the reader as interesting or effective (Samway, 2006).
Mark Up Method	Students read and mark the texts with the following coding system: a "." to show that a concept or fact is already known, a "?" to show that a concept is confusing, a "!" to show that something is surprising, a "+" to show an idea or concept that is new, or an "x" to show something they disagree with or that challenges their way of thinking. Then they can share the rationale for their thoughts with a partner (Adapted from Echevarria et al., 2017).

Structured Writing Activities

Just as with reading activities, the first step in creating structured writing activities is to determine the purpose for writing. Specifically, we want to define how the writing task will help students gain an understanding of the objective. For example, if a science objective requires students to explain the differences between states of matter, the writing assignment needs to support that goal.

The second step for creating a structured writing activity is to ask, "Can my students successfully complete the writing task on their own?" If the answer is no, then supports that lead to writing independence need to be put in place. Modeling is a very effective strategy, and all students benefit from explicit modeling of the writing task. In a think-aloud strategy, we verbalize the thinking that goes on in the writer's mind while writing. This helps establish a common ground for writers and demystifies the writing process for students. Alternative strategies include establishing prior knowledge and using sentence frames. Providing sentence and paragraph frames gives students more language to use to begin writing. The more ideas and language students have before they begin to write, the more independent and confident they become as writers.

Lastly, decide on a specific writing strategy, structure, or process that reinforces the content goals. Writing activities range from informal written responses on sticky notes to formal research reports with presentations.

SCAFFOLDS TO SUPPORT WRITING

» Sentence stems

» Paragraph frames

» Shared writing

» Providing writing samples

» Outlines and graphic organizers

Here are some examples of structured writing activities:

RAFT (Role, Audience, Format, Topic)

This writing strategy enables students to write from various points of view, using different genres, topics, and audiences. It works well in all subjects, but especially in Language Arts. RAFT (Fisher & Frey, 2007) is highly engaging for students in content-area classrooms because it injects creativity into sometimes dull concepts. RAFT stands for Role (the perspective the student takes), Audience (the individuals that the writing is addressing), Format (type of writing that will take place), and Topic (the subject of the writing). We can select all four categories for students or allow students to self-select some or all of them. Some examples include:

Class	Role	Audience	Format	Topic
Language Arts	Myself	Classmates	Narrative	Summer vacation
Math	Triangle	Other shapes	Persuasive speech	Why I can't be a square
Science	Sir Isaac Newton	Students	Letter	Laws of motion
Social Studies	Native American chief	Younger tribesman	How to	Survive (find food, shelter, clothing, protection)
Physical Education	Fifth-grader	First-grade class	List	Expectations in gym class

Expert Writing

In Expert Writing, students take on the role of "expert" for a given topic, concept, or unit of study. To introduce this strategy effectively, have all students find an area in which they are already an expert (making macaroni and cheese, coding, recording YouTube videos, etc.) and then complete the expert writing process with that topic before moving to academic concepts.

When they're ready to tackle an academic topic, students brainstorm (individually or with partners) a list of questions that someone would ask an expert of a particular topic/field. For example, an expert on the Peaceful Revolution of 1989 might be asked the following things: Who was involved in the Peaceful Revolution? Why was there a conflict? How did the situation come to a resolution? During the unit of study or individual lesson, the student takes notes on the answers to those questions.

Then the student writes an explanation or description of the topic or concept including all of his or her "expert knowledge." Expert writing works across all content areas and grade levels. Including an Expert/Novice Conversation (see p. 79) during the brainstorming phase helps generate more ideas.

Roving Paragraph Frames

The activity Roving Paragraph Frames combines listening, speaking, reading, and writing in an interactive format. Students engage in a series of short conversations, each of which culminates in creating a new sentence. The collection of sentences created eventually forms a paragraph. This strategy can be used as a warm-up activity, a transition midway through a class period, or a closure to review the day's concepts and learning.

Directions:

1. To begin the activity, give your students a sentence stem to be completed in writing. Sample: "When describing Abstract Expressionism, it is important to remember_____."

2. Give students a set time to think about the stem and write out their complete sentences.

3. Ask the students to stand up with their paper and pencils when they have completed the written sentence.

4. Have the students "rove" around the room and find a partner.

5. Ask students to read their writing to one another. The first person reads their complete sentence (stem + response). The second person listens and then reads their own complete sentence.

6. The partners then collaborate to write a new sentence that begins with a new stem, such as "In addition, _____." They can "borrow or steal" each other's responses if they are different, or they can create a new sentence.

7. Once sentence number two is complete, partners raise their hands or stand back to back. The key here is to incorporate total response signals to indicate to the teacher that the task is complete. Now they are ready to rove again!

8. Have the students find new partners and repeat the entire process with the second partner. It is crucial to instruct students to take turns reading every-thing they have written so far and listening to each other's sentences. This validates student responses and encourages the use of listening and speaking skills.

9. After reading their first two sentences, students write a third sentence with the stem "Also, ____."

10. To conclude, have students repeat the process one last time, roving to find their final partners. Once each partner reads his or her sentences aloud, ask students to write the final sentence using the last stem, "Finally, ____." At this point, each student should have a well-constructed paragraph in hand, with transitions and complete thoughts.

Other examples of Structured Writing Activities:

Writing Activity	Description
Dialogue Journal	A journal that is exchanged between the student and teacher or between two or more students that focuses on academic topics. The language used in the journal should be content-focused and academic.
Letters/ Editorials	Students write letters and editorials from their own points of view or the point of view of a character in a novel, a person from history, or a physical object (sun, atom, frog, etc.).
Read, Write, Pair, Share	This strategy encourages students to share their writing and ideas during interactions. Students read a text, write their thoughts using a sentence stem, pair up with another student, and share their writing.
Draw and Write	Have students draw visuals to represent their understanding of content concepts from their reading. Students then write descriptions of their drawings.

WHAT RESEARCH SAYS

Structured reading and writing strategies are essential to creating deep comprehension of new learning. When used effectively, they help create processes that students can access to make sense of new material. Research suggests that implementing the 7 Steps can have a positive impact on English learners' performance on reading assessments. In Phase I of The 7 Steps Study (see p. 107), overall reading score averages for English learners were significantly higher for treatment groups above corresponding control groups. Reading and writing allow students to articulate their understanding of content, clarify thinking, and then reflect and explore ideas to promote a deeper understanding of the text. Data suggests that readers' proficiency and comprehension are greater when reading more culturally relevant stories that support student reading development, foster a love of reading, help students form positive identities, and broaden their social consciousness (Freeman-Green et al., 2021; Kibler & Chapman, 2019). Reading strategies allow students the chance to engage in metacognition as they self-monitor their understanding of the text.

Structured writing strategies also help to build metacognitive tools for learners. Fountas and Pinnell (2001) stated that these strategies help students understand the informational text structure. According to Graham et al. (2018), the use of structured reading strategies can also foster students' writing performance. Their meta-analysis of 54 studies—including over 5,000 students from pre-k through 12th grade—found the effect of reading interventions on student writing to be statistically significant, with treatment groups outperforming their controls on writing proficiency. The effects of using a structured write-to-learn activity in content areas other than language arts also improved learning in science, social studies, and math across elementary, middle, and high school students (Graham et al., 2020). In a study of fifth- and sixth-grade students, findings indicated that students who received explicit writing instruction and individual writing tasks significantly outperformed those students who received no writing modifications to their individual practice on post-treatment assessments, revealing the effectiveness of structured writing instruction (De Smedt & Van Keer, 2018). Explicit writing structures have illuminated success for learners at all levels of language learning. Freeman-Green and colleagues (2021) identified writing structures such as the use of self-regulatory strategy development, mnemonic devices, and graphic organizers that demonstrate effectiveness for culturally and linguistically diverse and exceptional students.

Step it UP!

Once your students have learned to participate in structured reading and writing activities, STEP IT UP to provide opportunities for them to think critically and creatively while reading and writing. One way this can be done is by incorporating higher-order thinking into writing prompts.

Teachers might use questions and sentence stems to get students to analyze, evaluate, and create a Ticket Out. For example:

> » Middle school social studies: Based on what we just learned about Andrew Jackson, would you say he acted ethically or unethically? Why? (I think Andrew Jackson acted ____ because ____.)

> » Elementary math: How is addition different from subtraction? (Addition is different from subtraction in that ____.)

> » High school science: What might happen if thermal energy did not transfer between the ocean and atmosphere? (If thermal energy did not transfer between the ocean and atmosphere, ____.)

Writing from a different perspective in a Character Journal entry (see p. 139) is another way to have students demonstrate critical and creative thinking skills. In a Character Journal, students write from the perspective of a person, place, thing, or idea. Students have to understand a particular concept well to take on such a perspective, which can serve as an effective way to assess content knowledge. For example:

> » How would a right angle explain its relationship to a triangle?

> » How would a eukaryotic cell explain the differences between itself and a prokaryotic cell?

> » How would a noun describe its relationship to the other parts of a sentence?

> » What would a Patriot say to a Loyalist?

Frequently Asked Questions

 1 How do I create and include higher-level reading and writing prompts?

The Step it Up box on the previous page discusses how to begin helping students think at the higher levels both when reading and providing written responses. One approach to doing this is through incorporating higher-order thinking in writing prompts for activities such as Ticket Out and Character Journal.

Teachers can also assign writing tasks in the classroom or online to help students begin to develop argumentative literacy, i.e. the ability to make and understand reasoned arguments. One structure for doing this is Written Conversation, which can be a great framework in which to embed higher-order thinking and reasoning.

Written Conversation

In this strategy, students engage in either passing notes back and forth or typing in an online chat.

Here are the steps:

1. Identify two points of view. The two perspectives do not have to be opposed to each other. For example, we might have reasons a farmer would support a tariff and reasons a businessman would support a tariff.

2. Have students brainstorm a list of key vocabulary relevant to the topic.

3. Pair the students and assign each student one of the perspectives. Each pair has one piece of paper.

4. Explain to the students that the notes they are going to write must meet the following requirements:
   a. Each student writes one complete sentence each time the note is passed.
   b. Sentences must have capital letters and correct punctuation.
   c. Students are to use as many words as they can from the vocabulary brainstorm list or the word wall, and these words must be circled (or highlighted on screen) when the activity is concluded.

5. Give the students a sentence starter to begin the written conversation and have one partner write a sentence representing their point of view. When finished, have students pass the note to their partners or simply let their online partners know that they have finished writing their responses.

6. Have students read what their partners wrote and then write a response. Students continue to pass the note back and forth, writing about their topic for ten minutes.

7. Select volunteers to read their written conversation to the class when the activity is finished.

Here are some examples of higher-level prompts to use in written conversations:

» An elementary student might take the perspective of Goldilocks, while another takes the perspective of the three bears to discuss whether or not Goldilocks was actually trespassing on the bears' property.

» A middle school student might take the perspective of Alexander Hamilton, while another student takes the perspective of Thomas Jefferson to debate the formation of a national bank.

In both of these activities, the teacher can provide stems such as these, which help students argue from each point of view:

» In my opinion__ should have _____ because ___.

» The reasons I think _____ are ___ and ___.

» Points to consider regarding __ are ___ and _____.

» On the other hand, a reason against ___ is ___. This is proven when __.

» I respectfully disagree with _____ because _____.

Another way teachers can help students develop argumentative literacy is by assigning writing tasks in which students persuade an audience.

For example:

» In reading, students can write advice telling the main character how to solve the problem before they read the climax of the story.

» In social studies, students might write about a current event to persuade support for solving a community problem.

» In science, students could write a discussion between friends on the plummeting numbers of insect species.

» In math, students might write to someone who is opening a savings account about why compound interest is better than simple interest.

Students can write from a particular point of view in the context of the Letter/Response activity (see p. 145), in which students write letters about a particular topic, exchange the letters, and then write responses to the letter they received. After receiving the response, students discuss whether they agree or disagree with how the individual responded to their letters. Stems such as the following can be used for this activity:

Sentence Stems for Letter	Sentence Stems for Response
Dear _____, I'm writing this letter to ask you about...	Dear _____, Thank you for your letter...
I'm curious about why you decided to...	I'd like to begin by explaining why...
How did you feel when...	I felt...

② Why do most structured reading activities require students to write?

To measure the effectiveness of structured reading activities, we must assess student comprehension. The thinking that occurs when students read is an internal process, and to assess student comprehension, we must create a path for making that process visible.

Writing about the text provides a way for students to demonstrate their understanding of the reading. An alternative way to measure reading comprehension is to have students discuss what they have read. Students can discuss their reading in groups or with the teacher, using structured conversations or sentence stems. In essence, it isn't enough to ask students to read; they must read and make sense of the text. When students respond in writing or conversation, it is easy to see what they have learned.

③ What can I do to help my struggling readers and writers achieve success during structured reading and writing activities?

We all have students who encounter difficulty in the classroom. To help these struggling students, it helps to teach with an "I do, we do, you do" mentality. This approach is a simplified way to foster student independence. Let's look at the Draw and Write structured writing activity as an example. Our first step could be to explicitly model the activity. Begin by reading a portion of a text with your students. Afterward, complete the following steps:

> » (I do.) Draw a picture presenting the key ideas in the text, and then write sentences that explain your drawing.

> » (We do.) Read another short portion of a text and have the students draw a picture with you by adding small images that represent different ideas. Next, with your students, co-create sentences to clarify the picture.

> » (You do.) Students draw and write independently.

Some students may only need one explicit example and one shared example in order to succeed independently. In contrast, other students may need multiple modeled examples and many practice opportunities to master the activity.

Another thing many teachers do to help students achieve success with structured reading and writing activities is use students' independent work time to pre-teach concepts and vocabulary for the next day's lesson. This gives struggling students additional exposure to the material they will need. Three other ways to offer support are:

> » by providing an already completed example of the reading or writing task for students to reference,

> » by using adapted texts, and

> » by maintaining a dialogue journal with each student to identify and correct specific areas of confusion.

How can I incorporate these activities and get my students ready for the state assessments in reading and writing? There isn't enough time to do both.

It is easy to think of test prep and high-interest activities as mutually exclusive, but they are just the opposite. Making structured reading and writing activities an integral part of your lessons provides students with consistent opportunitiesto practice the same critical-thinking skills required of them on state tests.

For example, determining a character's motivation and summarizing a narrative are both common state standards. We can teach to these standards using a structured reading activity and at the same time prepare students for a standardized test. Whether we choose high-quality literature or use test preparation materials (such as released state tests), we can incorporate the language of the assessment in our instruction.

To measure student comprehension, we can continue to ask questions in a multiple-choice format; we can also have students participate in a structured reading activity like Somebody-Wanted-But-So (see p. 88). Students only have to select an answer choice to complete a multiple-choice question, but they must write thoughtful, individual responses based on their understanding of the narrative for the Somebody-Wanted-But-So activity. Using a structured reading activity will invite higher-order thinking skills, and in the end, this kind of activity better prepares students for state assessments. In fact, continued practice in thinking critically about a text and engaging in structured writing will increase a student's ability to write comprehensively and cohesively.

"These 7 Steps truly are applicable for any grade level or content area and can be implemented by any adult in the school ecosystem. By implementing these, every educator and leader can understand concrete ways to support multilingual learners while maintaining high levels of rigor for all."

Carly Spina
District EL Bilingual Instructional Coach

How do I implement Step 7 in a virtual environment?

Virtual classrooms provide unique opportunities to have students frequently engage in content-area reading and writing. Regular use of short, quick reading and writing tasks that students can perform in shared online platforms can keep students engaged and focused. Multilingual learners can often thrive when reading and writing in virtual environments when they make use of translation features and have opportunities for one-on-one/small group interaction with the teacher through breakout rooms or chat features.

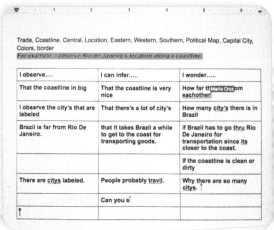

- ☐ Students can complete shared reading and writing tasks (such as partner reading) on online, interactive platforms.
- ☐ Teachers can select a narrator to read responses out loud.
- ☐ Multilingual learners can use translation features.
- ☐ Many websites offer cross-curricular content that have great scaffolds for English learners embedded in them.
- ☐ Teachers should be explicit about different ways students can read with support. ⟶

Part 2

The 7 Steps Study: Research on Program Effectiveness

by Sharon R. Goldman, EdD

s teachers, administrators, and district leaders, we have all tried many ways to improve education for English learners (ELs). There are countless initiatives in use across the country, but few offer definitive solutions that improve education for linguistically diverse students. Figuring out which methodology will meet your students' needs is often a time-consuming and quite difficult initiative. The study discussed in this chapter is dedicated to finding out how effective the 7 Steps instructional delivery model is for teaching ELs and how the teachers and administrators implementing it feel about the program. There is a great deal of current literature that supports the use of this language-rich, interactive classroom pedagogy.

WHAT RESEARCH SAYS

It is well known that the barriers linguistically diverse students face can severely limit their academic success. According to Goldenberg (2013), "It is an inconvenient truth that we lack the knowledge to fully prepare teachers to help many of their ELs overcome the academic achievement gaps they face" (p. 10). In the United States, there are more than 5 million students attending K-12 schools who are not proficient in English, and current literature identifies an achievement gap in reading and math between native English speakers and English learners (Bailey & Carroll, 2015; Barrow & Markman-Pithers, 2016; Cheung & Slavin, 2012; Hemphill & Vanneman, 2011; Lavery et al., 2018; Suárez-Orozco & Suárez-Orozco, 2015; Wilcox & Jeffery, 2014). Nationwide data also shows that ELs underperform their English-speaking peers in all fifty states (Migration Policy Institute, 2018; Office of English Language Acquisition, 2019; Nation's Report Card, 2019).

New content standards require an even more in-depth application of content knowledge from students to expand what counts as "meaning-making" in content-area classrooms (Grapin, 2019), and there is evidence that ELs suffer even further once they reach secondary schooling in the United States (Santibañez & Gándara, 2018; Schneider, 2019).

Texas schools have the second largest population of English learners in the country, comprising over 800,000 ELs in K-12 classrooms (Rolle & Jimenez-Castellanos, 2014; National Center for Educational Statistics, 2019). For the past 20 years, there has been a significant gap in academic achievement for ELs in Texas (Nation's Report Card, 2017; Office of English Language Acquisition, 2019), as evidenced by significantly lower standardized assessment scores and high dropout rates across the state. When comparing the percentage of students who do not meet grade-level achievement goals in math and reading, the gap progressively widens between students with limited English proficiency and English-speaking students as they move from fifth grade to eighth grade and into high school (Texas Education Agency, 2019). According to current data, ELs in Texas have far less success meeting grade-level proficiency in both math and reading in middle school, with less than 10 percent reaching grade level expectations by the end of the school year (Nation's Report Card, 2019; Slama, 2012).

Published research across the country calls for new strategies to teach ELs, highlighting the importance of providing content and language support in all classrooms (Garcia, 2014; Hopkins et al., 2015; Leith et al., 2016; Suárez-Orozco & Suárez-Orozco, 2015; Weinburgh et al., 2012). The 7 Steps to a Language-Rich, Interactive Classroom methodology offers a simplified, step-by-step approach that has had a positive impact on academic achievement for ELs (Goldman et al., 2021; Lara & Seidlitz, 2013).

The Research Design

One of the critical goals of systems in education is to reduce the gaps between marginalized students and students who are members of the dominant group. Today the English-speaking culture is still dominant in schools across the United States, and there are specific structures and behaviors that limit full participation of marginalized groups. Using a transformative worldview for evaluating *The 7 Steps Study* allows us to focus on the minority population of ELs being served by the program. This study addresses issues regarding equitable instruction for ELs through both the use of and research on the 7 Steps methodology. It evaluates the 7 Steps as structurally inclusive practices that encourage equitable inclusion of students in classroom conversations. The study began with an understanding of how

important it was to find out if the 7 Steps methodology improves access to content and promotes academic success for non-English speaking students. The hope was that the study would provide evidence supporting the notion that this language-rich practice contributes to the creation of more equitable learning environments for linguistically diverse students.

The research team looked at several aspects regarding how this program actually affects academic success for English learners in 7 Steps classrooms. The detailed plan we created allowed us to look at different sets of data to find out what was working. The following research questions were developed to set the stage and guide the study:

» What effect does the implementation of the 7 Steps methodology have on student performance in content and language assessments?

» Does the use of the 7 Steps instructional delivery model significantly improve the academic success of English learners in traditional classrooms?

» How does the fidelity of implementation affect student outcomes on standardized assessments?

» What do teachers and administrators think about the use of the 7 Steps in their schools?

PHASE I: 2019 Cohort Assessment

Preliminary Findings

PHASE II: 2021-22 Treatment Year Data Collection

Secondary Findings & Analysis

PHASE III: 2022-23 Post-Treatment Data Collection

Final Study Findings & Cross-Case Analysis

With these in mind, it was decided to use a mixed methods approach combining qualitative and quantitative data analyses to determine overall effectiveness of the 7 Steps program on EL student proficiency. A three-phase plan was developed to focus the research (see Figure 1, p. 111). By design, quantitative data was analyzed in the first phase to establish initial results, followed by qualitative analysis of classroom implementation and teacher input, and then additional assessment data from subsequent school years.

During Phase I, baseline and treatment year data were collected to measure the difference between treatment and control groups and the effect size for students taught with the methodology. The data set included scores from the State of Texas Assessment of Academic Readiness (STAAR) in math and reading proficiency and the Texas English Language Proficiency Assessment Systems (TELPAS) measuring reading, writing, listening, and speaking to determine English language acquisition levels. Data sets were collected from almost 1,000 English learners in treatment classrooms from the 2014-15 through 2018-19 school years. Preliminary findings showed a positive relationship between the use of this instructional delivery model and effectively teaching ELs, resulting in educationally significant effect sizes across all assessment areas. A cross-case analysis from multiple districts in the next two phases will be compiled to further validate these findings. Combining results from all phases of this study will provide rich, complex results to identify the effectiveness of teaching ELs with this inclusive framework.

This longitudinal study is further outlined in Figure 2 (see p. 112), summarizing the methods for collecting and reporting data for all phases of the study. This sequential design for data collection and analysis begins with Phase I for the following outcomes:

1. Student data identifying changes in reading and math scores

2. Mean comparisons between treatment and control groups in math and reading

3. A comparison of proficiency in English language acquisition skills between treatment and control groups

4. Correlation of student exposure to the treatment and resultant assessment scores

During final study analysis, data from all participating districts will be used in a parallel, partially mixed sequence that will be independently analyzed for effect size and correlated in cross-case analyses. This will be combined with the qualitative data to analyze the overall effectiveness of implementing 7 Steps as a definitive methodology for addressing the achievement gap between English learners and English speakers.

Data Analysis

During Phase I of this study, assessment criteria were explored to determine academic success based upon growth and mean score attainment between treatment and control groups for students currently classified as English learners with limited English proficiency. Annual assessment data on math, reading, and language skills was collected from the 2015 through 2019 school years. This included sets of data from 992 of these English learners, analyzing two years of pre-treatment baseline data and three years of treatment data. Cohorts were established by participation in their first treatment year and followed through subsequent years of assessment results. Exceptions to inclusion in the analyses were made for English learners enrolled for their first year in U.S. schools and students who took advanced math or reading classes.

Phase II will include a qualitative analysis reviewing implementation of the pedagogy through the use of an observational tool (see Figure 3, p. 113) to explain the relationship of data collected to the framework of this study. Teacher feedback will also be collected during the second phase to obtain qualitative information from those participating in the study who are applying the 7 Steps in their classrooms. A correlation of this data to the quantitative analyses conducted will help to further understand the implications of 7 Steps instructional strategies being used to benefit ELs in the middle school math and reading classrooms.

Upon completion of Phase III data collection, subsequent analyses will occur to obtain an in-depth understanding of the impact this teaching methodology has on student performance and will include: a correlation of teacher implementation levels to student outcomes; a review of findings from all participating districts; comparisons of differing outcomes using demographics to analyze differences; regression analysis of number of treatment exposures to student outcomes; cross-case, in-depth analyses; and subsequent findings related to the 7 Steps structure and the relationship of particular steps to improvements in student proficiency in math and language acquisition skills.

The 7 Steps Study Phase I Findings

The following findings highlight the educationally significant differences found in the data. To evaluate the overall effectiveness of the 7 Steps pedagogy, scaled score averages on end-of-year assessments were analyzed of all English learners identified with limited English proficiency (LEP). These students were grouped by grade level across three school years from 2016-17 through 2018-19. During the first year of the treatment, only 6th graders participated in 7 Steps classrooms. In the second year, 7th grade was added, and 8th graders became part of the treatment group in 2018-19. This resulted in much higher numbers of sixth graders participating over the course of the three years; collectively one-third of all LEP students were included in classrooms implementing the 7 Steps treatment.

Analysis of the effect size that the 7 Steps treatment had on students participating in the program revealed positive results for all grade levels. The STAAR Math assessment scores were collected from 317 students in the treatment groups and 660 students in the control groups. The largest treatment effect size was found in math scaled score averages, ranging from small, but educationally significant in 7th grade (0.17), to moderate in 6th grade (0.30), and a statistically significant impact in 8th grade (0.48). Overall, the program had a positive effect on improving proficiency in math and promoting LEP student achievement above the mean.

Notable results were also seen for reading cohorts in all three grades. The STAAR Reading assessment scores were collected from 312 students in the treatment groups and 683 students in the control groups. Though the effect sizes were not as substantial as those in math, they also represent findings showing small, but educational significance in 6th grade (0.20) and 7th grade (0.11) to having a moderate

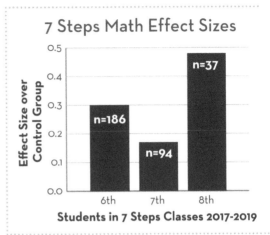

7 Steps Math Effect Sizes

Effect Size over Control Group

n=186 (6th), n=94 (7th), n=37 (8th)

Students in 7 Steps Classes 2017-2019

7 Steps Reading Effect Sizes

Students in 7 Steps Classes 2017-2019

Effect Size Over Control Group

impact on 8th grade (0.26) reading proficiency. These overall effect sizes found that it was beneficial for LEP students to be in the 7 Steps classrooms as a means to improve their academic proficiency in both reading and math. Further, the effect sizes increased over time for almost every cohort in both subjects, indicating that there is a positive correlation between improved academic success for English learners and the application of this methodology.

Understanding effect size in educational statistics is slightly different than understanding scientific measures on a binary scale, as in the "Either it works, or it does not work" types of measurement. Any program that allows students to improve their proficiency during one school year has the potential to shift their performance trajectory for all the school years that follow. The list to the right compiled from scholars in the field of education research (Kraft, 2020; Hattie, 2015; Schagen & Hodgen, 2009) can be used to consider the effect sizes found in the preliminary review of the 7 Steps instructional delivery model as well as effect sizes in other studies on educational programs.

This research on the use of effect size in educational research points to several distinct considerations for interpretation. The effect that can be elicited over time to change student trajectories may be greatly impacted by even the smallest margin. With this in mind, the data found during a review of Phase I data was promising.

Findings from the STAAR math assessment scaled scores showed the majority of treatment groups performed above their control groups, and while not all findings show statistical significance, almost all groups outperformed control groups by considerable margins.

The 6th grade treatment cohorts, when averaged across all three years, had math scaled score averages that were 30.85 points higher than their corresponding

control groups. Most noteworthy were the results from the second and third years of treatment implementation. In the 2018 analysis, students in the first treatment cohort scored an average of 83.9 points higher than controls on their end-of-year math assessment and 45.75 points higher in 2019 with an effect size of 0.48. Additional analysis from 2019 math data showed that 8th graders who had two years of treatment exposure versus the control group found significant interaction between grade level and number of exposures with an effect size of 0.91. When comparing any treatment versus any control, treatment groups scored an average of 31.9 points higher than controls.

2017–2019 STAAR Math Averages

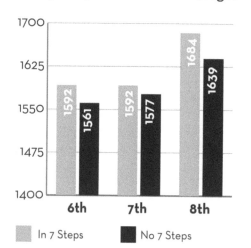

2017–2019 STAAR Reading Averages

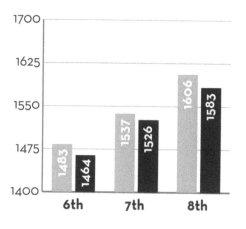

STAAR reading data showed similar results, with most treatment groups outscoring their control groups, though differences were not always statistically significant. Figure 5 (see p. 115) shows the average scaled scores achieved by each grade and cohort in reading, with treatment students across all grades and for most years outperforming their controls. In 2018, the first cohort of 7 Steps students had growth resulting in an increase of 0.40 effect size during their second year. When comparing any treatment to any control in 2019, the results varied, with the 6th grade treatment group having one of the highest effect sizes during the third year of the study (g=0.24). The overall effect size in 7th grade cohorts showed less significant differences, yet 8th grade reading assessment data showed the highest effect size (g=0.26) and the biggest difference in average scaled scores, with the treatment group having an average of 23.8 points higher than the control group. Applying a comparison to control for the differences in sample sizes using Hedge's g, the scores and standard deviations were pooled to reveal significant weighted mean differences by grade level and subject on STAAR math and reading (see graph on p. 108).

The level of English language acquisition indicated on the 2017-2019 TELPAS for all students who participated in the treatment showed overall composite scores to be higher than their controls (See Figure 5). When comparing data from the third year between treatment and control groups, there was a statistically significant difference in writing proficiency between the two groups (p=0.046), with treatment groups scoring on average 0.425 points (10.6%) higher than controls. In the comparison of any treatment versus any control, there was statistical significance in writing across the groups (p=.001) where students in all treatment groups scored an overall average of 0.28 points (7%) higher than controls. ELs in 7 Steps classrooms outperformed their control groups in writing across all grades (see Figure 5, p. 115), and consistent results were also found in all areas of the English language acquisition assessment. Using 6th grade as the largest group across all tested years as a sample for comparison, the treatment groups (n=186) versus control groups (n=364) found that those who participated in the treatment classrooms outperformed the control group across all years on 87% of TELPAS tested areas,

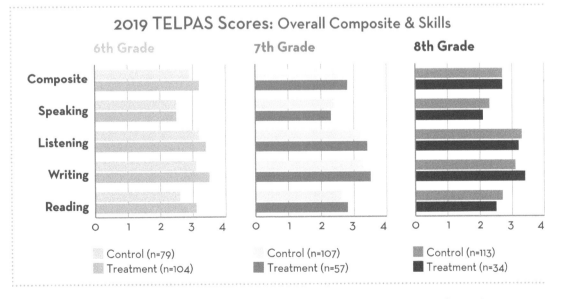

2019 TELPAS Scores: Overall Composite & Skills

including reading, writing, listening, and composite scores. Similarly, in 2019, when all grades were included in the study, treatment groups consistently outperformed their controls in most tested areas (see p.109). This data indicates a strong correlation between the implementation of 7 Steps pedagogy and the acquisition of English skills above their peers who were not involved in the treatment.

Discussion

Preliminary findings from the first phase of this study identified a positive relationship between the use of the 7 Steps methodology and increased academic proficiency for English learners in middle school math and language skills. The impact was greatest in math classes across all treatment cohorts, and the research team surmised that the addition of language instruction into math content areas was a key factor in promoting this success. Language assessment scores were higher for treatment cohorts, and students who participated in more 7 Steps classrooms over the course of the three years often showed continued improvements in their proficiency on academic assessments in math, reading, and English language skills.

Overall effect sizes in math showed that over 70% of the control groups performed below the mean of the treatment group, with an overall 1increase in effect size of 0.30 from sixth grade to 0.48 in eighth grade. This seems to indicate that the more years teachers had to develop their 7 Steps implementation system, the higher were the resultant student scores. It is also clear that students more significantly outperformed their peers when participating in 7 Steps classrooms with teachers who had more years of experience implementing the methodology. The overall effect sizes indicated increasing effectiveness in both math and reading instruction, with scores rising on STAAR

assessments from the first to the third year. In reading there was a medium effect size, which resulted in a greater than average influence on student outcomes. Performance on annual TELPAS assessments, measuring English language skills, indicated that the treatment groups outperformed controls in a large majority of tested areas and average composite scores across all three years, with statistically significant growth in writing across all grades.

Patterns that emerged from analysis of the assessment data highlight the overall impact of implementing 7 Steps methodology as a beneficial pedagogy for teaching EL students. The importance of relating the findings from this study to the overall impact that this methodology may have on the EL population is paramount when considering the notion of balancing educational access for marginalized student groups. Since the gap between ELs and native-English speaking students widens in middle school–and this methodology has shown to decrease this gap–it is imperative to further explore its implications.

We are very encouraged by the positive results, which allow for the generalizability of these findings to promote the use of the 7 Steps to teach English learners everywhere. The approach gives educators the ability to reach EL student populations through socially just initiatives that break down barriers caused by instructional delivery models that are unable to accommodate for linguistic diversity. The ultimate goal is to improve education by creating educational structures, processes, and discourses that will positively affect speakers of other languages, embracing the significant EL population in our schools and across our communities.

* For more information regarding this study, please scan the QR code to access *The 7 Steps Study* materials.

Research Charts & Figures

FIGURE 1. *The 7 Steps Study* Data Collection Protocol

	Procedure	**Products**
PHASE I: 2019 Cohort Assessment	1. Identify 7 Steps Cohorts 2. Collect 2 years baseline data on STAAR Math & Reading and TELPAS 3. Collect past year's treatment data on STAAR Math & Reading and TELPAS 4. Conduct analyses of student data and cohort trajectories 5. Correlate data by grades, courses, schools, & district 6. Evaluate significant changes	» Cohort identification » Baseline data sets » Cohort trajectories » Treatment data » Proportional difference » Mean comparisons » Binomial significance » Overall effect size
Preliminary Findings		
PHASE II: 2021–22 Treatment Year Data Collection	7. Collect 2020-21 school year treatment data on STAAR Math & Reading and TELPAS 8. Conduct 4-5 observations in each 7 Steps Math & Reading classrooms 9. Distribute qualitative teacher questionnaire in Spring of 2020 10. Analyze student data from treatment year 11. Correlate data across all years by grades, courses, schools, & district	» Treatment data » Proportional difference » Mean comparisons » Median difference » Value relationships » Observation results » Variable correlations » Data relationships » Control group values » District-wide analyses
Secondary Findings & Analysis		
PHASE III: 2022–23 Post-Treatment Data Collection	12. Collect 2021-22 school year post-treatment data on STAAR Math & Reading and TELPAS 13. Analyze 5-7 years of Cohort data 14. Correlate data across all years by grades, courses, schools, & district 15. Correlate data across all districts 16. Compare findings to Texas state data on ELs & Limited English Proficient Students	» Post-treatment data » Final school analyses » Final district analyses » Treatment vs. Control » Cross-case correlation » Statewide comparisons » Effectiveness evaluation » Implications of the 7 Steps methodology for teaching ELs
Final Study Findings & Cross-Case Analysis		

Research
Charts & Figures

FIGURE 2. *The 7 Steps Study* Data Collection Flowchart

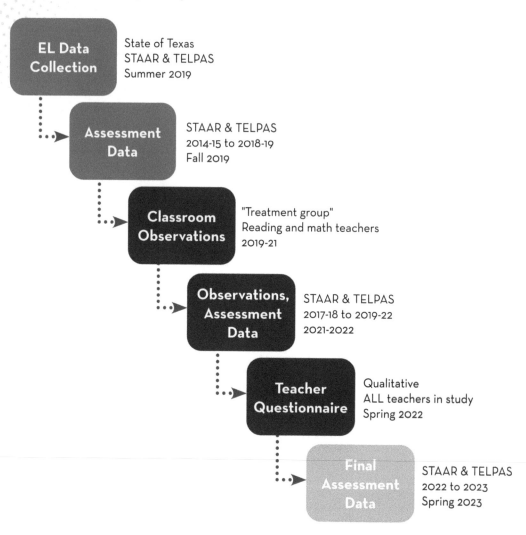

EL Data Collection
State of Texas
STAAR & TELPAS
Summer 2019

Assessment Data
STAAR & TELPAS
2014-15 to 2018-19
Fall 2019

Classroom Observations
"Treatment group"
Reading and math teachers
2019-21

Observations, Assessment Data
STAAR & TELPAS
2017-18 to 2019-22
2021-2022

Teacher Questionnaire
Qualitative
ALL teachers in study
Spring 2022

Final Assessment Data
STAAR & TELPAS
2022 to 2023
Spring 2023

PHASE 1 - Quantitative Data

Collect 5-7 years of assessment data

STAAR Reading & Math and TELPAS

Analyze baseline data for all cohorts

Correlate & compare "treatment" data

PHASE 2 - Qualitative Data

Establish 7 Steps teacher lists

Collect classroom observation data

Complete teacher questionnaires & student surveys

Code & analyze all qualitative data

PHASE 3 - Cross-Case Analysis

Collect "post-treatment" data from all districts

Analyze longitudinal data from all study groups

Compare to District, State, and National norms

Correlate results with qualitative findings

FIGURE 3. *The 7 Steps Study* Observation Protocol

School: _____ Teacher: _____ Date/Time: _____

Instruction Observed (check all that apply):

☐ Whole Class(teacher led)   ☐ Student Groups/Partners   ☐ Independent/ALL

Step	Teacher	Y	N	Students	Y	N	Notes	Instruction
1	Systematically supports students to avoid the use of "I don't know" when calling on non-volunteers (alternative response, reference visuals, rephrase questions, redirect, use pause or facial cue, etc.)			Most respond to questions posed by teacher when called on avoiding the use of "I don't know"				Whole Class only
2	Prompts use of complete sentences, redirecting students who use incomplete sentences			Most respond verbally using complete sentences with or without prompting				Whole Class only
3	Uses randomization system throughout the lesson			Participate in randomization system				Whole Class only
4	Checks for understanding of content using total response signals (written or ready-to-share response, choice or ranking, etc.)			All participate in checks for understanding				Whole Class only
5	Uses visuals/vocabulary strategies that develop academic language related to objectives			Make use of visuals/vocabulary strategies that develop academic language related to objectives				ALL
6	Provides structured opportunities for academic conversation through explicitly planned student interaction using sentence stems or academic vocabulary			Most participate in structured conversation utilizing academic vocabulary				WC & SG/P
7	Assigns structured reading/writing tasks explicitly planned to build academic language related to objectives			Participate in structured reading/writing tasks				ALL
	TOTALS							

7 Steps Implementation Rating: (circle one)
0 = No evidence of 7 Steps   1 = Some evidence of 7 Steps   2 = High degree of 7 Steps evident

Research
Charts & Figures

6th Grade STAAR Math

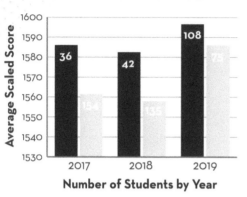

Average Scaled Score

Number of Students by Year

6th Grade STAAR Reading

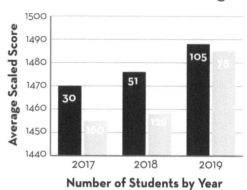

Average Scaled Score

Number of Students by Year

7th Grade STAAR Math

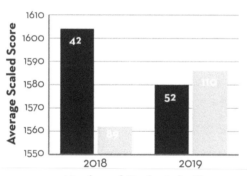

Average Scaled Score

Number of Students by Year

7th Grade STAAR Reading

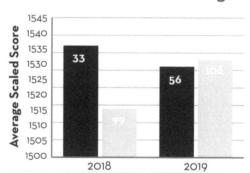

Average Scaled Score

Number of Students by Year

8th Grade STAAR Math

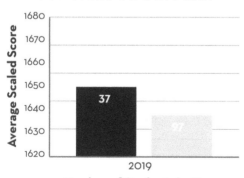

Average Scaled Score

Number of Students by Year

8th Grade STAAR Reading

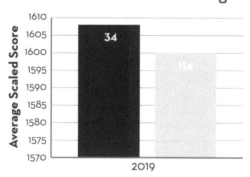

Average Scaled Score

Number of Students by Year

Numbers in bars indicate how many students were in each group

Treatment

Control

FIGURE 5. *The 7 Steps Study* TELPAS Writing Scores by Grade: Phase I

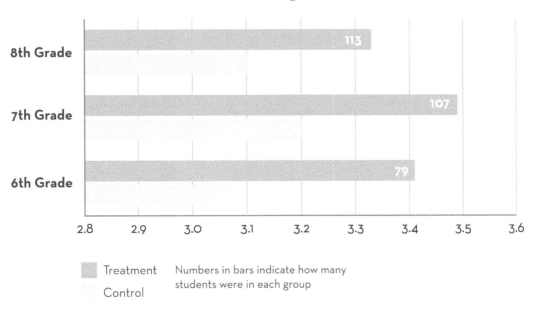

2019 TELPAS Writing Mean Scores

(Bar chart)

- 8th Grade: 113
- 7th Grade: 107
- 6th Grade: 79

X-axis: 2.8, 2.9, 3.0, 3.1, 3.2, 3.3, 3.4, 3.5, 3.6

Legend:
- Treatment
- Control

Numbers in bars indicate how many students were in each group

TIPS

Principles For A Language-Rich Interactive Classroom

The 7 Steps are based on four key ideas, or TIPS, that lay the groundwork for a successful language-rich, interactive classroom. When we plan instruction using TIPS as a guide, our students benefit. By creating lessons with total student participation, incorporating content-specific vocabulary, promoting literacy and language development, and scaffolding for struggling students, we establish a framework for success. Using the 7 Steps and the TIPS framework, we have the tools to ensure that our students are involved, articulate, and successful.

Total Participation

This principle is clear: all students will participate. This means that every student, during every activity, is involved in listening, writing, speaking, or reading. To make a class truly language-rich and interactive in a way that can help students grow in their use of language, educators must provide students with comprehensible input and low-stress opportunities for output. Comprehensible input happens every time students hear or read challenging words and phrases that they are able to understand because of their background knowledge and context clues. Low-stress opportunities for output happen whenever students have a chance to speak and write authentically using new language in a non-threatening environment. Language development cannot happen without comprehensible input and low-stress opportunities for output; rather, we as teachers must create classrooms that establish total participation during activities that involve listening, speaking, reading, and writing.

The type of participation may vary from student to student depending on his or her ability and the task at hand, but non-participation is not an option in a language-rich, interactive classroom. The key to securing 100 percent participation from our students is to create an environment where students want to be involved.

Incorporate Content-Specific Vocabulary

The vocabulary used within most classrooms is largely centered on specific content concepts. Our goal is to have students learn and use this vocabulary in each lesson in clear and effective ways. For example, we want students in science class to use science vocabulary in the proper context when speaking and writing. While it can be difficult to determine which words to teach (especially if our students begin with limited vocabulary knowledge) there are methods to use. Dutro and Moran (2003) suggest thinking about vocabulary in terms of brick and mortar words to guide us.

Brick words are content-specific vocabulary. In seventh grade math class, for example, some brick words are three-dimensional, polygon, and prism. Brick words for second grade social studies class might include natural resource, producer, and consumer. While these words are found in the glossary of a content textbook, it is often necessary to teach brick words explicitly, using vocabulary strategies such as Marzano's Six-Step Process (see p. 60).

Mortar words—commonly found in academic contexts—are words that connect, describe, or help us process the brick words. Mortar words are not found in any glossary, but textbooks and tests use these words regularly. Examples of mortar words are: similar, between, finally, disagree, possibility, and based upon. We do not need to teach the meaning of these words explicitly, but we do need to increase student comprehension of mortar words by simply using them as part of our conversations and including them in our sentence stems.

Instead of asking a student, "What do you think about what you just read?" reframe the question using mortar words and ask, "Based upon the passage, what is your opinion of what you just read?" The more students hear and use new words and phrases, the more they will use them. Repetition is the key.

Promote Literacy and Language Development

During both planning and executing lessons, we have a goal that is twofold: build literacy for students while helping them grow in their language development. The word "literacy" has a variety of meanings. In this context, literacy refers to the comprehension of the important ideas and key concepts of any given content area. It's helpful to think of phrases like "math literacy" or "historical literacy."

In order to promote content literacy for students, we, as teachers, have to provide the students with content-area texts. We can then focus on providing multiple opportunities for students to interact with the material using critical thinking skills like evaluating, generalizing, and classifying information. Clear content and language objectives enable students to expand their language development as we build in time within instruction for students to consistently listen, speak, read, and write about key content concepts.

Scaffolding for Struggling Students

It is important to provide support that gives all students the self-confidence and independence they need to succeed. Being prepared to help struggling learners who encounter difficulty means examining our learning environment as well as our classroom procedures. In our classrooms, we can create supportive environments by filling the walls with visuals that are teaching tools, by arranging desks so that students can collaborate, and by teaching

students how to use resources within the classroom.

Following the pattern of "I do, we do, you do" or "I use the language, we use the language, you use the language" can be a helpful way of structuring how we scaffold for our students. During instruction, we can model what to do when students get stuck, and we can encourage students to use a buddy for clarification. In addition, teaching problem-solving skills will diminish the struggle some students have and make it easier for them to learn.

Content and Language Objectives

How to Write a Content Objective

A content objective is a clear statement that establishes what students will learn or be able to do by the end of each lesson. It forms the goal for the lesson and serves as a guide for teaching and learning in the classroom. Content objectives specify which key ideas or concepts are the focus of instruction and at what depth students will learn them.

When writing content objectives, teachers use curriculum standards to provide a concrete guide for deciding what concepts to teach. Similarly, Bloom's Taxonomy can provide language that explains how deeply the concept is taught. Many teachers are familiar with Bloom's Taxonomy, which has been used to help classify thinking into lower-order and higher-order levels. *Know* and *Understand* require lower-level, less rigorous thinking. Some refer to *Apply* as lower-order thinking, and others refer to it as higher-order thinking. However, *Analyze, Evaluate,* and *Create* are always recognized as requiring higher-order thinking.

Effective content objectives have three characteristics: they correspond with curriculum standards, they match one level of Bloom's Taxonomy, and they are measurable. Follow the step-by-step process below to write a content objective that meets all of these characteristics.

One: Identify the key idea or concept to be taught.

Using the curriculum standards for the grade level and subject area, determine the key idea or concept to teach. Many districts also have a pacing guide or scope and sequence document that helps teachers decide the order in which to teach concepts.

Two: Determine the appropriate level of Bloom's Taxonomy.

Determine at what cognitive level you want students to learn the key concept. Once that is determined, then select a verb that matches that level. For example, during introductory lessons, you may simply want students to identify basic concepts, and in later lessons, you may want students to apply and evaluate the new concepts. Bloom's Taxonomy (see p. 120) provides a structure to label the level of thinking.

Three: Select appropriate activity.

Decide what students will do in order to show that they understand the idea and have learned the key concept. This activity should be observable and measurable; that is, students will show that they understand the concept and to what level they understand. For example, "Students will identify the main idea and three details found in chapter seven," is observable or measurable, whereas, "Students will learn about the main idea and detail," is not.

Four: Write the content objective.

Write a complete sentence that tells the students these three things:

1. The key concept they are going to learn

2. The level of depth of understanding

3. The observable and measurable activity or activities they will complete

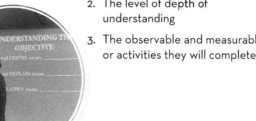

Levels of Bloom's Taxonomy

Remember	Understand	Apply	Analyze	Evaluate	Create

Sample Verbs to Include in Content Objectives

Remember	Understand	Apply	Analyze	Evaluate	Create
Choose	Classify	Act	Break down	Appraise	Adapt
Count	Cite	Assess	Characterize	Argue	Build
Define	Conclude	Change	Classify	Assess	Collaborate
Describe	Convert	Chart	Compare	Choose	Combine
Draw	Describe	Collect	Contrast	Conclude	Communicate
Find	Discuss	Compute	Correlate	Criticize	Compile
Identify	Estimate	Construct	Debate	Critique	Compose
Label	Explain	Contribute	Deduce	Decide	Construct
List	Generalize	Determine	Diagram	Defend	Create
Match	Illustrate	Develop	Differentiate	Determine	Design
Name	Interpret	Discover	Discriminate	Evaluate	Develop
Quote	Make sense of	Dramatize	Distinguish	Interpret	Devise
Recall	Paraphrase	Draw	Examine	Judge	Facilitate
Recite	Predict	Extend	Focus	Justify	Formulate
Record	Report	Implement	Illustrate	Predict	Generate
Reproduce	Restate	Interview	Infer	Prioritize	Individualize
Select	Review	Include	Limit	Prove	Initiate
Sequence	Sort	Inform	Outline	Rank	Integrate
State	Summarize	Instruct	Point out	Rate	Invent
Tell		Participate	Prioritize	Support	Make up
Write		Predict	Recognize	Validate	Model
		Prepare	Research		Modify
		Produce	Relate		Negotiate
		Provide	Separate		Organize
		Relate	Subdivide		Perform
		Report			Plan
		Select			Produce
		Show			Propose
		Solve			Rearrange
		Transfer			Revise
		Utilize			Rewrite

Examples for How to Write a Content Objective

Second Grade Language Arts

One: Identify the key idea or concept.	Identify statements as opinion and fact. (Curriculum Standard)
Two: Determine level of depth of understanding.	Understand level of Bloom's Taxonomy with "sort" as the verb of the objective.
Three: Select appropriate activity.	Sort sentence strips describing *I Wanna Iguana* as opinion or fact
Four: Write the content objective.	Students will be able to sort example sentences describing *I Wanna Iguana* as opinion and fact.

Eighth Grade Math

One: Identify the key idea or concept.	Select and use appropriate order of operations to solve problems and justify solutions. (Curriculum Standard)
Two: Determine level of depth of understanding.	Application level of Bloom's Taxonomy with "apply" as the verb of the objective.
Three: Select appropriate activity.	Solve multistep word problems involving everyday activities.
Four: Write the content objective.	Students will be able to apply addition, subtraction, multiplication, and division skills to solve multistep word problems involving everyday activities.

Fifth Grade Social Studies

One: Identify the key idea or concept.	Explain the reasons for and the right provided by the 15th amendment to the U.S. Constitution. (Curriculum Standard)
Two: Determine level of depth of understanding.	Understand level of Bloom's Taxonomy with "explain" as the verb of the objective.
Three: Select appropriate activity.	Create an interview-based news show in groups of three.
Four: Write the content objective.	Students will be able to explain the reasons for and the right provided by the 15th amendment to the U.S. Constitution by creating a news show in groups of three.

Ninth Grade Biology

One: Identify the key idea or concept.	Compare and contrast prokaryotic and eukaryotic cells. (Curriculum Standard)
Two: Determine the level of depth of understanding.	Analysis level of Bloom's Taxonomy with "create" as the verb of the objective.
Three: Select appropriate activity.	Complete a Venn diagram.
Four: Write the content objective.	Students will be able to compare and contrast prokaryotic and eukaryotic cells by completing a Venn diagram.

Sixth Grade Language Arts

One: Identify the key idea or concept.	Include dialogue that develops the plot in imaginative stories. (Curriculum Standard)
Two: Determine level of depth of understanding.	Application level of Bloom's Taxonomy with "include" as the verb of the objective.
Three: Select appropriate activity.	Write two sentences with dialogue.
Four: Write the content objective.	Students will be able to include two sentences of dialogue to develop the plot in an imaginative story.

Equine Science Elective

One: Identify the key idea or concept.	Evaluate various nutrition plans for horses. (Curriculum Standard)
Two: Determine level of depth of understanding.	Evaluate level of Bloom's Taxonomy with "evaluate" as the verb of the objective.
Three: Select appropriate activity.	Orally describe the strengths and weaknesses of specific horse nutrition plans.
Four: Write the content objective.	Students will be able to identify proper nutrition requirements by evaluating various nutrition plans for horses.

How to Write a Language Objective

A language objective is a clear statement that explains what language skills or processes students will use during a lesson. Many teachers of English learners use language objectives as a way to focus language development for their students. Language objectives communicate the specific ways that students will listen, speak, read, or write. English Language Development/ English Language Proficiency (ELD/ELP) standards can provide a concrete guide for writing language objectives.

Effective language objectives have three characteristics: they support the lesson's content, they align with English Language Development/English Language Proficiency (ELD/ELP) standards, and they are measurable.

To create a language objective, write a language goal for the students that includes the following:

1. The language domain through which they will show their learning
2. The connection to the content
3. The specific words, phrases, or stems they will use

Use the sentence frame below to ensure all three components are included in the language objective:

Students will _____(verb aligned to a specific language skill)

by _____ (content-area connection to the content objective)

using ___ (specific words, phrases, stems, or skills).

Here are some examples of language objectives:

Content Objective	Language Objective
Students will be able to explain the reasons for the right provided by the 15th amendment to the U.S. Constitution.	Students will orally share with a partner the reasons for the adoption of the 15th amendment using the vocabulary words *ratify* and *citizenship*.
Students will be able to compare and contrast prokaryotic and eukaryotic cells.	Students will explain in writing the similarities and differences between the two types of cells using their Venn diagram and these sentence stems: Prokaryotic and eukaryotic are similar in that... Prokaryotic and eukaryotic are different because...
Students will be able to apply addition, subtraction, multiplication, and division skills to solve an original multi-step word problem involving an everyday activity.	Students will be able to write a multi-step word problem using the phrases *best represents, total amount,* and *least to greatest.*
Students will be able to identify and use dialogue in a class created story.	Students will be able to construct two sentences of dialogue in an imaginative story using correct punctuation.
Students will be able to identify proper nutrition requirements by creating a diet plan for a horse.	Students will describe in writing the proper nutrition for a horse using this sentence stem: A horse should/should not eat...because...

The following chart lists examples of language objective starters:

Language Objective Stems Aligned to Cross-Curricular Student Expectations*

Listening

Students will...

- recognize correct pronunciation of...
- recognize sounds used in the words __ and ___.
- identify words and phrases heard in a discussion about...
- check their understanding by.../seek help by...
- use _ (media source) to learn/review ...
- describe general meaning, main points, and details heard in...
- identify implicit ideas and information heard in...
- demonstrate listening comprehension by...
- identify relationships between sounds and letters by...

Speaking

Students will...

- pronounce the word __ correctly.
- use new vocabulary about __ in stories, pictures, descriptions, and/or classroom communication.
- speak about...using the sentence stems...
- speak about...using the words__ and _.
- share in cooperative groups about___using...
- ask and give information about __ using the words __ and ___.
- express opinions, ideas, and feelings about __ using the words/phrases...
- narrate, describe, and explain ___ using...
- use formal/informal English to discuss...
- respond orally to information from a variety of media sources about...

Reading

Students will...

- recognize the words/phrases __ and ___.
- use prereading supports such as_ to understand...
- read materials about __ with support of simplified text/visuals/word banks as needed.
- use visual and contextual supports to read...
- show comprehension of English text about ___ by...
- demonstrate comprehension of text read silently by...
- show comprehension of text about __ through basic reading skills such as (decoding, using background knowledge, fluency).
- show comprehension of text/graphic sources about __ through inferential skills such as (making connections, drawing conclusions, making inferences).
- show comprehension of text about __ through analytical skills such as (evaluating information, judging, classifying, analyzing).

Writing

Students will...

- learn relationships between sounds and letters when writing about...
- write, using newly acquired vocabulary, about...
- edit writing about _with a focus on (complete sentences, correct verb use, or using a variety of simple and complex sentence types).
- use simple and complex sentences to write about...
- write using a variety of sentence frames and selected vocabulary about...
- (narrate, describe, or explain), in writing, about ___ using...

* These stems are written based on the Texas English Language Proficiency Standards.

Higher-Order Thinking Skills

with MLLs using the 7 Steps

Not only is it possible to build higher-order thinking in the language-rich classroom, but doing so enhances both academic achievement and English language proficiency for multilingual learners (MLLs). Any student who is acquiring a second language can greatly benefit from the inclusion of higher-order thinking in lessons that promote the use of content-rich vocabulary. In a study of the effects of higher-order thinking on student achievement, Teemant et al. (2016) found that when teachers used higher-order thinking methods in their lessons, students who were acquiring English made significant gains in both language arts achievement and English proficiency. Nunan (2015) discussed how students could be involved in their own learning processes through the use of metacognitive tasks that are integrated into the classroom environment. Studies such as these have demonstrated the value of increasing the level of cognitive challenge when teaching multilingual learners.

Developing language and cultivating thinking is not an either-or proposition. Teachers can incorporate strategies that promote higher-order thinking within the very instruction that promotes language acquisition for MLLs. Getting students to use content-specific vocabulary is merely the beginning. In order to create language-rich environments that further build students' capacity to engage in higher-order thinking, educators can coach students to take risks and go beyond just using the language, to truly developing their own thinking and language processing skills. The sections below outline three key ways teachers can enhance language learners' linguistic and cognitive development: critical thinking, creative thinking, and problem solving.

Critical Thinking

There are many definitions for and ways of categorizing critical thinking; however, all acknowledge judgment and decision-making as important skills. Ennis, author of the Cornell Critical Thinking Test (1987), defines critical thinking as "reasonable, reflective thinking that is focused on deciding what to do or believe" (p. 10). This definition was expanded upon at the 8th Annual International Conference on Critical Thinking and Education Reform: "Critical thinking is the intellectually disciplined process of actively and skillfully conceptualizing, applying, analyzing, synthesizing, and/or evaluating information gathered from, or generated by, observation, experience, reflection, reasoning, or communication, as a guide to belief and action" (Foundation for Critical Thinking, 2019).

Current education experts working to improve schooling for MLLs continue to be strong proponents of developing critical thinking skills. The authors of *The Translanguaging Classroom* (Garcia et al., 2017) highlight the significance of metalinguistic processes in which students make choices about how and why to use language. These choices allow language learners to see the world through their own creative and critical multilingual perspectives. By making choices, language learners engage their brains in higher-order processes and become adept at thinking critically about both the language and content of their lessons. To limit their high potential for processing at this level–by avoiding questions that provide opportunities for critical thinking–would merely serve to hold them back solely because of a perceived language barrier.

Creative Thinking

It is important we teachers recognize that multilingual learners use creative thinking and apply higher-order cognitive abilities all the time. As such, it is our reponsibility to further develop these skills so that students may realize their true potential.

Sometimes referred to as the "Father of Modern Creativity," E. Paul Torrance based his Torrance Test of Creative Thinking (1969) on the dimensions of divergent production defined as fluency, flexibility, originality, and elaboration. This notion has been implemented across many educational disciplines for years and is further developed in his book entitled *Guiding Creative Talent* (2018).

Fluency refers to the ability to produce a large number of ideas, while flexibility refers to the capacity to generate different categories of ideas. For example, students are told by the teacher to brainstorm a list of "things that are red." Students who are able to generate a large number of things that are the color red exhibit fluency, and those who come up with the idea of "read," as in "I read a book," are able to be flexible and shift categories. Originality, another component

Components of Creative Thinking	
Fluency	ability to produce a large number of ideas
Flexibility	ability to generate different categories
Originality	ability to produce a novel or original idea
Elaboration	ability to add details to an idea to enhance it or make it more useful

of creative thinking, is possessing the ability to produce a novel or original idea. Students who generate a new idea that successfully meets the criteria with a product that differs from most of their peers are showing originality. The final component is elaboration in which students add details or enhance an idea in a way that makes it more useful or interesting. Students who answer all the "5 W's and How" in the development of a plan are being elaborate.

Bakr (2004) found that after presenting instruction to increase these creative thinking skills of English learners at a preparatory academy over a 10-week period of time, the students who received this instruction significantly outscored the control group on both creativity (fluency, flexibility, originality, and elaboration) and achievement.

Creative Thinking Question Stems

What connections can we make between _____ and _____?

How can we find out more about _____?

What do you predict will happen if _____?

What can you conclude about _____? Why?

Creative Thinking Sentence (Response) Stems Categorized by Proficiency Level:

Level 1: I think __ will __.

Level 2: I predict __ will happen next because __.

Level 3: I hypothesize __ will happen if ___.

Level 4: Based on the information in ___, it seems that ___ will most likely happen when __ because ___.

Problem Solving

Providing tools and structures to address problem solving offers a means to engage multilingual learners in higher-order thinking skills. Alex Osborn and Sidney Parnes (1985) developed a model of Creative Problem Solving that encompassed both critical and creative thinking through a series of sequential actions to solve a problem. This practice was developed further by Miller et al. (2001) to help teachers apply this model in the classroom by expressing a more plain-spoken version:

The first two actions require critical thinking. The third (generating ideas) requires creative thinking. The last two (selecting and strengthening solutions and planning for action) require both critical and creative thinking. Wang (2019) studied the effects of applying the Creative Problem Solving model in an L2 classroom through writing tasks and found students indicated a positive feeling about the effects of these tasks on facilitating their English skills, creative thinking, classroom participation, and interaction.

Identify the Goal, Wish, or Challenge

1. Gather Data
2. Clarify the Problem
3. Generate Ideas
4. Select and Strengthen Solutions
5. Plan for Action

Problem Solving Question Stems

How would you approach the problem _____?

What are possible solutions for _____?

What is another way you could solve _____?

What is proof that _____?

Problem Solving Sentence (Response) Stems Categorized by Proficiency Level:

Level 1: The information I use to ___ is ___

Level 2: ___ proves that ___

Level 3: ___ helped me determine ___ is a ___

Appendix

Appendix A

Developing a Language-Rich, Interactive School

The 7 Steps can transform a classroom culture into a language-rich community where students feel confident, intelligent, and included. When implemented consistently across an entire school, the 7 Steps can have profound and lasting effects on students' mastery and versatility with language. Imagine walking the halls of a school in which, in every single classroom, students can be heard and seen speaking and writing in complete sentences, participating equitably with total response signals, and using academic vocabulary in small-group and whole-class settings. And imagine the experience of a single student, many times throughout the day in every subject and class, listening attentively to his teachers and peers while speaking, reading, and writing using complex, content-specific language.

Supporting the development of a language-rich, interactive school involves two instructional leadership actions: (1) instructional coaching that focuses on teachers' strengths and helps them cultivate a pedagogy centered on language-rich instruction; and (2) facilitation of collaborative planning within professional learning communities.

Coaching Teachers on the 7 Steps

Effective coaching requires a cycle of reflection between a teacher and an instructional coach in which the coach observes the teacher's implementation of a strategy and then both reflect together about the experience, concluding with collaborative goal setting for the next observation (Knight, 2008). This goal can be the implementation of a new strategy or a refinement of the current strategy. As the teacher and coach continue progressing through cycles of observation and reflection, the teacher's pedagogical skills, and simultaneously students' learning and engagement, will grow measurably.

When coaching the 7 Steps, coaches can support teachers in achieving the broader goal of a language-rich classroom by focusing on consistent implementation of Steps 6 and 7. These steps are multifaceted, and they require the use of several of the 7 Steps to implement. The three tables on the following pages show a typical pathway of progression in the implementation of Structured Conversations (Step 6), Structured Reading (Step 7), and Structured Writing (Step 7). While not every teacher will follow this exact trajectory (for example, some teachers may implement a randomization system before they begin asking students to speak in complete sentences), the tables can help teachers and coaches have a clear idea of which steps are being used, which are not, and how the use of these strategies relates to students' use of language.

Step ⑥ Structured Conversations

Level	Teacher Action(s)	Observable Student Actions	
		In-Person	**Virtually**
	Asks questions to the class (volunteered response)	Few students respond while others are silent	Few students respond while most others stay muted (other students might have videos off or display no evidence of engagement)
2	Refers to visual or text before asking questions **AND** Provides sentence stem before asking questions **AND** Has students use a response signal to indicate readiness before asking questions	Student engagement apparent in students looking at visual/text and using response signal	Students use response signal in video or refer to visual/text in responses
	Uses a randomization system to call on students **AND** Provides options for the students if they do not know	Different students routinely answer different questions; they rarely say, "I don't know"	Different students routinely unmute to answer different questions; they rarely say, "I don't know"
4	Allows students to talk to each other before being called upon **AND** Specifies who will speak to whom (elbow partner, group, etc.) and who will speak first (person #1, person with longest hair, etc.)	All students speak with each other about each question while using content-specific language	All students speak with each other about each question in breakout rooms or other online sharing platforms while using content-specific language
	Asks open-ended questions **AND** Asks at least three questions per lesson	Frequency of students' content-specific language is at least equal to frequency of the teacher's content-specific language	

Step ⑦ Structured Reading

Level	Teacher Action(s)	Observable Student Actions	
		In-Person	**Virtually**
1	Assigns students reading tasks	May be unclear whether students are actively reading and/or comprehending the text	
2	Communicates purpose of reading to students directly aligned to task following reading	Students refer to reading in post-reading task	
3	Uses reading strategies such as the following: Having student identify unfamiliar or new (e.g., vocabulary) words **OR** Having students make predictions before reading **OR** Having students make annotations or highlight during reading	Students actively interact with the text before and/or during reading by making annotations, highlighting, or underlining words or phrases	Students actively interact with the text before and/or during reading by making annotations, highlighting, or underlining words or phrases, evident by showing on video or by typing annotations in e-documents
4	Has students discuss predictions, annotations, and new learning before and/or after reading Structures student conversations (see "Step 6: Structured Conversations" table) about text with think time, sharing directions, and sentence stems	Students make references to the text in structured conversations	Students make references to the text in breakout rooms or other online sharing platforms
5	Provides multiple reading opportunities throughout each lesson with structures to have students interact collaboratively with the reading	Students obtain new information from reading at least as frequently as from listening to the teacher	

Step (7) Structured Writing

Level	Teacher Action(s)	Observable Student Actions	
		In-Person	**Virtually**
	Assigns students writing tasks	Participation and engagement with writing varies with no clear quality standards	
2	Provides sentence stems for writing **AND** Requires students to use key vocabulary in writing and/or examples	Students incorporate sentence stems and key elements into their writing, improving consistency and quality of work	
	Communicates expectations for high-quality writing (e.g., by showing examples of high-quality and low-quality work)	Students avoid elements of low-quality writing (such as overuse of unclear words and lack of elaboration) and include some elements of high-quality writing	
4	Has students verbally share writing with each other and provides opportunities for them to revise their responses Structures student conversations (see "Step 6: Structured Conversations" table) about writing with think time, sharing directions, and sentence stems	The gap between the highest-quality response and the lowest-quality response in a lesson decreases, and student responses improve overall over time	
	Provides multiple writing opportunities throughout each lesson with structures to have students interact collaboratively with the writing	Students regularly write short or elaborate responses throughout the lesson	Students regularly type out short or elaborate responses throughout the lesson

To foster a strengths-based coaching conversation, coaches can use these tables as a central focal point to discuss what actions the teacher is currently doing well or consistently, and which actions might make good goals to try to implement and focus on in the next observation session. A coaching conversation might look like this:

COACH: I noticed that when you provided your students a sentence stem, they were more likely to answer in a complete sentence. What did you notice about how the students responded to the sentence stem?

TEACHER: I noticed that too, and I thought their answers were even a little bit more elaborate than usual. Some of the students didn't seem confident answering until they started saying the sentence stem, then it was like half the answer was already there for them.

COACH: That's an interesting point about their confidence. Maybe some students had not thought out their answers completely?

TEACHER: They might just need more think time. Especially my beginning and intermediate English learners, who I can tell are trying to process the language and the content of the question at the same time.

COACH: What would it look like if you had students use a response signal to show whether they're ready before you called on anyone?

TEACHER: I could try that. I could have students give me a thumbs up when they can answer the question, and then I'll call on someone after everyone puts their thumbs up.

COACH: Would you like me to focus on that in the next observation?

In this conversation, the coach has used the "Step 6: Structured Conversations" table to frame the teacher's strength (using sentence stems) and forge a connection to a next goal for implementation (using total response signals). Setting up coaching conversations by highlighting a teacher's strength to lead to creating a new goal empowers the teacher and creates a partnership between teacher and coach.

Facilitating Collaborative Planning Within Professional Learning Communities

Instructional leaders can support teachers by encouraging their use of this protocol and modeling how to collaboratively plan exemplar lessons. Additionally, creating campus-wide expectations for the inclusion of writing, discussion, and reading opportunities in every lesson can help emphasize the importance of intentionally planning out the language in language-rich lessons. The following planning protocol can ensure that teachers are able to create an exemplar lesson: a lesson with language output as the primary objective.

1. Write down an exit ticket for the lesson you want to plan to assess students' learning of the key ideas.

2. Write out an example of a high-level student response to the exit ticket in two to five sentences.

3. Underline two to four key vocabulary words in that response. In ELAR, this can be language-arts specific vocabulary, common words, examples, or instances of textual evidence.

4. Write down one or more discussion questions that either include one of the vocabulary words or elicit answers that include the vocabulary words. The following question stems are based on key vocabulary:

» How is ___ related to ___?

» How is ___ different from ___?

» How is ___ similar to ___?

» What is an example of ___? Why is this a good example?

» Why is ___ important for...?

» How would ___ change when...?

5. Write down sentence stems for each discussion question.

6. Plan out a slide/document/visual that shows the question, QSSSA structure, and any visuals for each discussion question.

7. Decide what the students will read (e.g., notes, book, article, visual, etc).

8. Decide what students will "pay attention to" or annotate while reading. This can be directly aligned to a discussion question that comes after the students read (e.g., students will underline examples of physical and chemical changes during reading, then discuss differences between physical and chemical changes after reading).

9. Decide what other scaffolds, instruction, or materials might be needed in this lesson.

PLC Planning Process for Language-Rich Instruction
Stephen Fleenor, PhD

Content Objective/ Learning Intention

• Which part(s) of the standard(s) do you want students to master?

• At what level of Bloom's Taxonomy?

Language Objective/Lesson Closure

• Which 2-4 vocabulary words should students be proficient in by the end of the lesson?

• What writing*/speaking prompt will assess student's master of the content <u>and</u> the vocabulary?

Class Discussions

1-3 open-ended questions for structured conversations that will help students:

• Process the content

• Practice using the vocabulary

Reading

• What will students read to help understand the content <u>and</u> gain contextual exposure of the language of the lesson?

• What will you instruct students to "pay attention to" or annotate while reading?

Direct Teach/ Lecture

What is the <u>minimum</u> direct explanation you need to do to make students successful when reading, writing, and discussing?

What sentence stems, visuals, and other supports (e.g., QSSSA) will ensure students are successful when reading, writing, and discussing?

* Students in grades 2-12 should be expected to write in complete sentences during the lesson.

Appendix B

Activities for the 7 Steps

The 7 Steps provide a simple road map for the high-quality education we want our students to have. Our goal is to create classrooms in which every student participates in academic conversations about great ideas. We want our students to see things from multiple points of view, and we want them to be able to express themselves intelligently and confidently.

This appendix contains examples of different activities that promote structured reading and writing opportunities. Also included is one extended activity called "Windows on History," which illustrates how to incorporate the 7 Steps in a lesson that spans multiple days in order to give students a deeper understanding of the content.

Activity Index

Artifacts and the Experts

In this activity, students take on various roles while examining objects or texts.

Before the lesson, the teacher selects an artifact that represents the topic of study. Artifacts may include items such as photographs, drawings, paintings, newspaper articles, mathematical models, tools, charts, graphs, or manipulatives.

The teacher then assigns roles to students as experts within a field of study relating to the artifact. The roles the teacher assigns depend upon the type of artifact. Some examples of possible expert roles are biologist, historian, professor, business owner, editor, mathematician, etc. Students take on their assigned roles and write questions/observations about the artifact from their "expert" perspectives. The class then discusses their observations as well as possible answers to some of the questions as a group.

In a math class, the teacher shows students a graph representing logarithmic growth of an investment. Students write various questions and observations about the graph from the perspective of investors.

In a science class, the teacher displays photographs and graphs showing the effects of weather changes on the migration of a bird population. Students can write various questions and observations about the photographs and graphs from the perspectives of ornithologists and climatologists.

In a social studies class, the teacher shows students a photograph of a family from the depression era. Students write various questions and observations about the photographs from the perspective of historians.

SENTENCE STEMS

» In our opinion, this is...

» The most significant feature of this __ is...

» We were wondering why...

» As __, we were curious about...

» One thing we noticed was...

» We suggest...

Building Block Cards

Description:

This activity (adapted from Zwiers, 2008) reinforces the concept that different kinds of words are needed to "build" academic understanding.

Dutro and Moran (2003) highlighted the idea that there are two types of academic language from each lesson: 1) the key terms or "big idea" vocabulary (content-specific words), and 2) the academic words that surround the key terms (non-content specific words). Content-specific words are usually bold faced or italicized in textbooks and teachers explicitly teach their meanings. Non-content specific words are general academic words that can be found in textbooks, tests, and conversations across all subject areas. They include transition words like *because*, signal words like *first* or *second*, and test-specific language such as *best represents* or *based upon*. Non-content specific words are often abstract, and without a clear definition, so the best way for students to learn these words is by using them. This activity gives students practice using the content-specific and non-content specific words they need to build academic understanding.

Directions:

List up to five key vocabulary words ("bricks") from a current unit of study.

1. Have students (in pairs or groups) record each term on individual index cards. These are the brick cards.

2. Ask students to organize the brick cards in a way that makes sense to them.

3. Ask students to discuss what words or phrases can be used to link the brick words together (you might offer a list of "mortar" words and phrases to support students during this activity).

4. Have students write the chosen words or phrases on "mortar" cards (or sentence strips) to cement the brick cards together.

EXAMPLE

Life Cycle of a Butterfly

CONTENT-SPECIFIC CARDS

metamorphosis · pupa · caterpillar · chrysalis · butterfly

List of NON-CONTENT SPECIFIC words/phrases:

transforms · next · grows · inside
first · changes into · begins
second · last · then · process
forms · eats · resting · stage
is called

POSSIBLE STUDENT RESPONSES:

1. A butterfly begins as a caterpillar and then a chrysalis forms. It is now called a pupa and then breaks out as a butterfly. This process is called metamorphosis.

2. Metamorphosis is when a caterpillar transforms into a butterfly. First, it is a caterpillar, then a pupa inside a chrysalis, and last a butterfly.

Bystander

Students play the role of witnesses to major historical events and take turns interviewing one another.

Choose a major historical event, and have students read about the event in small groups. Have students brainstorm a list of important facts, ideas, and incidents from the times surrounding the event. In pairs, students can act as a reporter and a bystander who witnessed the event. The reporter interviews the bystander using the sentence frames listed below.

SENTENCE STEMS

for Brainstorm
» The reporter might ask...
» (Character) probably believes...
» (Character) probably observed...

for Reporter in Dialogue
» We're standing here with...
» We've just learned...
» Could you tell me more about...?
» What were you doing when...?

for the Bystander in Dialogue
» When this started I was...
» I saw...
» I heard...
» I felt...
» I wondered...

Character Journals

In this activity, students read a selected passage or study a particular phenomenon. Then they summarize the information as a journal entry based on the point of view of a character or object.

After reading a selected passage or studying a particular phenomenon, students write a journal entry from the perspective of an individual or object within the newly learned material. The teacher provides sentence stems for support.

In a math class, students write a journal entry from the perspective of an individual in a word problem. For example, in a problem related to finding the perimeter of a fence, students write entries from the perspective of the fence builder who had to make decisions about finding the perimeter and building the fence.

In a science class, the teacher may have students write from the point of view of the liver describing its detoxifying role in digestion.

In a social studies class, after reading Sojourner Truth's speech entitled "Ain't I a Woman?" from the 1851 Akron, Ohio Women's Rights Convention, students respond with a character journal entry from the point of view of Sojourner Truth.

SENTENCE STEMS

» Today I...
» I can't believe what happened today...
» The most amazing thing happened...
» I will never forget...

Dead Word Cemetery

Teaching effective writing skills at all grade levels comes with many challenges, yet this simple approach to developing vocabulary has been used by teachers and students for years. In the activity, students create (and build upon) a word wall that *includes only the words they should avoid* in their writing.

Creating the Cemetery is a process you lead students through to build a monument on a classroom wall that expands their use of vocabulary in writing. Using a cemetery to "bury dead words" allows them to celebrate their word choices in writing and should evolve with each grade level. This can become part of the process when they write about what they are learning in your classrooms. Key components can include:

» Identify words that are "dead" - select low-level, over-used, or ambiguous words.

» Build the Dead Word Cemetery - create a word wall with tombstones and graveyard decor to ritualize the "passing" of words from the accepted vocabulary.

» Establish a routine for adding new words to the cemetery - decide points during the writing process when peer editors can offer "dead words" to the wall from their reviews (once a week).

» Develop lists of synonyms - students list better words to replace frequently abused vocabulary and write them on paper next to the dead words. This gives students support to replace dead words in their language.

Event/Response

Students respond to a short story or video clip from first-person perspectives.

In this strategy, the teacher reads a short story aloud to the students or provides an appropriate video clip for them to view. The reading or video clip could be about a historical/current event, about a novel or diary entry (e.g., The Diary of Anne Frank), or any grade-level appropriate literature.

After the reading or video, the teacher will lead a discussion with students to list the characters from the selection. The teacher will then assign a character to each student and ask for a written response using one of the sentence frames listed below. Students will be writing from their characters' points of view when they respond.

The sentence frames provided for this strategy lead students to write from the first-person point of view. This perspective-based writing strategy fosters a deeper emotional connection to the topic and between the student and the character.

SENTENCE STEMS

» Today I had to make a decision about...

» I survived today by...

» Let me tell you about the challenge I faced. I...

» I can't believe what happened...

Expert Advisors

In this perspective-based strategy, students are required to prepare a presentation for a historical character or a person who has a pivotal decision to make.

Directions:

This strategy requires students to move to a deeper cognitive level by examining multiple points of view and complex details regarding the issue at hand. Students take the perspective of "advisors" to ultimately support their "expert" presentation and advice using the sentence stems provided. This activity will usually take place after students have acquired familiarity with a topic, and it could involve extensive reading.

In a science class, students might assume the role of scientists who are considering whether or not to add an organism to the list of endangered species or whether or not NASA should spend money exploring the surface of Mars.

In a social studies class, students could prepare a presentation for members of the Second Continental Congress on whether or not to approve Richard Henry Lee's resolution for "free and independent" colonies. The students become the "experts" regarding the topic, and in their presentations, they advise the Congress about the upcoming vote.

SENTENCE STEMS

- » After much consideration, it is our opinion that you should...
- » One reason for our recommendation is...
- » You might also want to consider the fact that...
- » We took into account many factors, including...

Fortune/Misfortune

WATCH
Fortify Output
with Fortune/
Misfortune

Description:

This activity places students in the midst of the unit or topic they are studying. They write from a first-person perspective about the unit or topic and are faced with making decisions that may have a positive or negative effect. Students gain deeper levels of understanding because they are personally invested in the topic. Students take on the role of individuals who face advantages and disadvantages due to chance events and personal choices. This simulation enables students to experience the effects of personal decisions.

Directions:

Begin by reading and discussing a historical situation. Have students brainstorm a list of items they believe would be important to have if they were in that situation. For example, what would you want to have if you were a settler in Jamestown in 1607? What would you want to have if you were an American soldier in Vietnam in 1965? What equipment would you bring on a mission to outer space? What tools would you need when setting up an experiment to determine weather conditions? Students then make personal choices of six to ten things from the brainstormed list of items and copy them to their notebooks.

Students then write a short paragraph from the first-person point-of-view describing that day in history. Students use the list of items as they recount this day.

Next, have the class imagine possible fortunes and misfortunes that could happen in any of the historical situations. For example, what disasters could strike Jamestown? What good things might happen to the settlers? What could happen to an American soldier during wartime conditions? What problems might happen during the course of an experiment? The teacher writes these fortunes and misfortunes on index cards.

1. Have students read about and discuss (in the target language) a historical or real-life situation that reflects the current topic of study or unit of vocabulary.

2. Brainstorm a list of possible fortunes and misfortunes that could happen in the chosen situation. The teacher writes these possibilities on index cards.

3. Have students write short paragraphs from the first-person perspective describing a day in their situations.

4. The teacher selects a fortune or misfortune card randomly from the deck.

5. Ask students to write a new paragraph describing how they responded to the fortune or misfortune. Continue to draw additional fortune/misfortune cards, and have students write new response paragraphs.

6. Have students share their writing with partners or as a whole class to conclude this assignment.

SENTENCE STEMS

Brainstorm
» I'd want to have...
» One thing we'd need is...
» __ might be necessary to...

Typical Day
» Today began with...
» First, I...
» I also had a chance to...

Fortune/Misfortune
» It started when...
» Great news! Today...
» Bad news. Today...

Freeze and Speak

Description:

Students engage in a dialogue representing two points-of-view in front of an audience. Mid-discussion, students are asked to freeze, and one individual, "frozen in dialogue," is replaced by an audience member who continues the conversation.

Directions:

Freeze and Speak is an extension of T-Chart, Pair, Defend (see p. 155) with two students representing opposite points of view, in conversation in front of an audience. All students should participate in T-Chart, Pair, Defend prior to engaging in Freeze and Speak. This will prepare audience members to replace speakers and continue the conversation during the activity. The activity begins with two students engaging in T-Chart, Pair, Defend in front of the class. The instructor then directs the students in conversation to freeze and selects one student to exit the dialogue and sit down. The teacher then asks for a volunteer or randomly selects a student to replace the student who exited the conversation. The process continues with several students participating before the activity concludes.

Jury Decision

Description:

Students prepare a case for a prosecutor or a defendant and then take on the role of jurors who must make a decision in the case.

Directions:

After studying a significant court case, have the class brainstorm arguments in favor of the defense and arguments in favor of the prosecution. Divide the class in two and ask half of the students to write a closing argument in favor of the defense and half of the class to write a closing argument in favor of the prosecution.

Divide the class into groups of six. Each group of six will consist of three students who wrote closing arguments for the defense and three for the prosecution. The same students who wrote the arguments in favor of the defense and prosecution now sit in a circle and take on the role of jurors. They must try to come to a consensus about the case within a given period of time. Students can use the sentence frames below as they prepare their responses.

Debrief the activity as a class.

SENTENCE STEMS

for Dialogue

» We should/shouldn't...

» The best method is...

» No, I think the best method would be...

» I believe/don't believe...

Prosecution Stems

» You should find the defendant guilty because...

» The evidence shows...

Defense Stems

» You should find the defendant not guilty because...

» The evidence shows...

Juror Stems

» I think the defendant is guilty/not guilty because...

» The prosecution/defense clearly proved...

Learning Through Interactive Debate

Description:

Students participate actively in a debate as speechwriters, editorial writers, political cartoonists, and propagandists.

Directions:

This strategy helps students prepare to debate two opposing points of view. Select a particular topic to debate. Ideal topics will have clear pro/con sides that students can choose to debate (e.g., the American Revolution, the Protestant Reformation, the Civil War, the value of the Paris Climate Agreement).

1. Write the chosen topic of debate on the board. Make a "For" side and an "Against" side.

2. Have students make a list of reasons for and against the topic.

3. Display the prepared signs in different corners of the room: CHANTS, EDITORIALS, CARTOONS, and SPEECHES.

4. Have each student go stand by the activity of his choice.

5. Have students at each station count off as ones and twos. Students with one number will represent the "For" and the other students will represent the "Against." *Make sure each station has both ones and twos in order to represent all activities and sides during the debate.*

6. Have students use the brainstormed list of reasons to prepare cheers, editorials, cartoons, or speeches that represent their points-of-view.

7. When everyone is ready, have all the ones and twos face each other. The debate follows this order of activity: CHANTS, CARTOONS, EDITORIALS, and SPEECHES. Ones and twos alternate presenting.

8. Have both sides repeat their chants (with increasing enthusiasm) after the cartoons, the editorials, and the speeches.

9. After the debate, students participate in a secret ballot to determine who "won."

Letter to the Editor

Students write and respond to editorials from the perspective of various historical characters or individuals with perspectives on contemporary science and social studies topics.

Choose a controversial topic that aligns with your lesson objectives. As a class, list various perspectives on the topic and then brainstorm reasons to support each perspective.

Have students use their lists to write a letter to the editor of a newspaper reflecting their points of view. When complete, have the students exchange letters with a partner. Ask students to read each other's letters and then write their own letters opposing what they have read.

SENTENCE STEMS

Letter Sentence Stems

» Dear Editor, I'm writing concerning...

» It is my opinion that...

» We must remember...

» Finally, everyone must agree that...

Response Sentence Stems

» Dear Editor, In response to yesterday's letter concerning...

» The writer said...

» I disagree. It seems that...

» Have we forgotten...

Letter/Response

This activity is very much like a chapter review or paragraph summary with a small twist. In Letter/Response, students have a chance to inject their own curiosity and creativity while they use the target language in writing about real-world issues in the target culture and/or historical figures covered in the target-language curriculum.

After reading and discussing a historical era, piece of literature, or current event, students select characters to whom they would like to ask particular questions. Students then write letters (individually or in partners) to the individuals, asking them about their lives and important decisions they made.

1. Review current topic vocabulary with students.

2. Have students write a letter to the character about an issue or topic related to vocabulary covered in the curriculum.

3. Ask students to exchange letters with other students, and have them write a response to the letter they receive as if they were the character being written to.

4. Have students give the letter and the response back to the original writer, and have the two students discuss each other's responses.

SENTENCE STEMS

for Letter

» Dear __, I'm writing this letter to ask you about...

» I'm curious about why you decided to...

» How did you feel when...

for Response

» Dear __, Thank you for your letter...

» I'd like to begin by explaining why...

Museum Curator

Description:

Students prepare museum exhibits that illustrate lesson concepts and events.

Directions:

Before the lesson, prepare descriptions of the events or concepts you wish students to illustrate in the activity. Pass out the descriptions to students in small groups, and instruct them to prepare an exhibit that illustrates the meaning of the event or concept. Each group must have one or two speakers who can explain the exhibit to visitors. Exhibits may include sculptures, tableaux, illustrations, movies, slide shows, dioramas, or machines.

For example, in a science unit about reptiles, each group is given one topic to represent. The students make products such as a tableaux showing the extinction of dinosaurs, illustrations of various physical systems of reptiles, sculptures of particular reptiles, etc.

In a math class, teachers can have students create exhibits showing particular algorithms from a unit, or they can have students make exhibits modeling various word problems.

In social studies or language arts classes, teachers can have students create exhibits showing a variety of aspects of various texts and events.

When the students have finished their exhibits, they take turns wandering through the museum in groups. Half of the class can be museum visitors while the other half of the class demonstrates their exhibits.

SENTENCE STEMS

» This exhibit illustrates the idea of...

» Our exhibit shows the events of...

» (Event/Concept) is significant because...

News Show

Description:

Students take on the roles of producers of a news show reporting on a particular topic.

Directions:

Students prepare a "News Show" highlighting the chosen topic, including site location, studio guest interviews, and advertisements appropriate to the topic.

In math, a unit on fractions includes interviews with mathematicians to discover how people in different occupations solve various problems in their careers, using fractions or mixed numbers. In addition, students create advertisements using fractions or conduct on-location reports that highlight the setting of a particular word problem.

In social studies, students prepare a "News Show" regarding the nation's reaction to the Supreme Court's 1857 Dred Scott Decision. Interviews include responses from Dred Scott, members of the southern aristocracy, President James Buchanan, members of the Supreme Court, and abolitionists such as William Lloyd Garrison and Frederick Douglass.

SENTENCE STEMS

» Good evening, ladies and gentlemen, and welcome to...

» We are broadcasting tonight from...

» And now, a word from our sponsors...

» We now go on location to...

» Thanks, __. Turning to other news...

Perspective Choice

Students engage in dialogue from different perspectives as they take part in a group of six people who must make a choice.

After reading and discussing a topic in science or social studies, select a situation in which a group of six people must make a decision. As a class, write six different sentences that represent different perspectives on the same event using the sentence frames listed below.

For example, a family of medieval peasants, who are deciding whether or not to go on a pilgrimage, might come up with these perspectives:

1. "I think we should go on the pilgrimage because we've never been before."

2. "We ought to go because we will be able to visit some of the fairs and trade our goods."

3. "It would be a good idea to go because St. James' prayers have been known to be helpful."

4. "We definitely shouldn't go because I've heard towns in that area may have the plague."

5. "It's not wise to go because there are too many thieves along the road."

6. "I don't believe it's worthwhile to go because we have too much work to do here on the farm."

A group of scientists trying to decide how to increase productivity of farmland while conserving the local ecosystem might write these sentences:

1. "We need to prevent the next blight by diversifying our crops."

2. "We should put more artificial fertilizer on all the crops."

3. "We'll have more pollinators if we plant native flowers throughout the farms."

4. "We need to replace our current wheat crops with alfalfa, which have much longer, deeper roots to prevent soil erosion."

5. "What we really need are more trees throughout the farmland to attract birds that eat pests."

6. "We should dig irrigation ditches from the local lakes and ponds so crops have more water."

Number the perspectives one through six and have students form small groups of six, each student taking a different perspective. Students begin by reading a sentence from the board and then improvising a conversation based on their impression of what the characters might say. Students may repeat their conversations for the class. The class as a whole then discusses what might be the best choice for the group.

SENTENCE STEMS

» I think we should ___ because...

» We ought to ___ because...

» It would be a good idea to...

» We definitely shouldn't ___ because...

» It's not wise to ___ because...

» I don't believe it is worthwhile to ___ because...

Prop Box Improvisation

Students use props to create a verbal and visual representation of text.

After reading and studying historical content, students use a box of props to improvise and role-play assigned scenes in history.

For example, after reading and studying the voyages of La Salle, organize students into four teams. Each team will be responsible for developing an improvisation of one part of La Salle's journey. The challenge for each team is to use as many props as possible and to incorporate as many details, low-frequency words, and content-area words as they can in the improvisation/role-play. A narrator can be chosen to narrate each presentation. After each presentation, debrief by asking the audience to note the content details and the effective use of props. Provide the sentence frames below for students to frame their responses.

Suggested props for Prop Box: feathers, rope, binoculars, canteen, swords, scarves, artificial flowers, crosses, colored fabric, markers, construction paper, bandanas, canes, crowns, jewelry. (Note: swords, binoculars, crown, jewelry, etc. are all plastic toys.)

SENTENCE STEMS

» They demonstrated __ using...

» They showed __ with...

» I think they were trying to show __ using...

» They represented...

QSSSA

This strategy helps students use new target language structures and vocabulary during classroom conversations. The teacher asks the essential question that will be addressed in the conversation. Students give a predetermined signal when they are ready to respond and are given a sentence stem to use for their response. After sharing with a partner, students are chosen randomly to share with the whole group. In this activity, every student in the class participates using academic language, and it usually takes less than a minute to implement.

QUESTION: Ask the class a question.

SIGNAL: Ask students to give you a certain response signal when they are ready to answer the question.

STEM: Provide students with a sentence stem to use when answering a question.

SHARE: Give students an opportunity to share their responses with other students in pairs, triads, or groups.

ASSESS: Determine the quality of student discussions and the level of understanding by randomly selecting students to share out loud or by having all students write a response.

	Question	Signal	Stem	Share	Assess
Math	What are some important things to remember when deriving the equation of a parabola?	Raise your hand when you can complete this sentence –––>	One important thing to remember when deriving the equation of a parabola is... because...	Share in groups of three	Randomly call on students
Social Studies	Do you support Sam Houston's position on secession?	Place your hand on your chin when you can complete this sentence ––––>	I support/ oppose Sam Houston's position because...	Numbered Heads Together	Randomly select groups to respond
Science	What are some unusual characteristics of annelids?	Stand up when you can complete this sentence –––>	The most unusual characteristic of annelids is... because...	Share in groups of two	Randomly call on students
Language Arts	Do you think Esperanza's family made a wise decision?	Put your pen down when you can complete this sentence –––>	I think Esperanza's family made/ did not make a wise decision, because...	Share answers with several partners	Have students write their perspectives in journals

Research Team

Students become "experts" who research a topic and prepare presentations or products based on a social studies or science concept.

This perspective-based strategy is a long-term process, and the goal is to produce a presentation or product invented by a research team.

For example, students can be given the role of travel agents who prepare a brochure to convince their customers to travel to a particular location, or they can be scientists preparing an exhibit on endangered species for a local museum.

As an alternative, students can be given the role of World's Fair exhibition designers who research and prepare a cultural (wall panel) exhibit representing the religious, economic, social, geographic, artistic, and intellectual influences of a particular country. With multiple research teams in the classroom, several countries can be represented.

The following boxes provide sample directions for students:

Sample Directions

It is 1850. You have been hired as a private investigator by the United States government to research, investigate, and prepare a panel display showing the intricacies of the Underground Railroad. You are to include maps, routes, and cities that are major supply stations, individuals who are known supporters of the railroad, and other subtle codes and nuances used in this secret escape system.

Sample Directions

Following the COVID-19 pandemic, the United Nations has invited you, as part of an international team of epidemiologists, to advise governments on which pathogen might become the next pandemic. You have determined the most serious pathogens are the virus which causes Ebola, the protist that causes malaria, the fungus that causes blastomycosis, and the bacteria that causes cholera. You are researching the symptoms of each disease, how the pathogens reproduce and transmit, and the infection and death rates. Based on your findings, you are to provide a formal recommendation to the United Nations about which pathogen is most detrimental to the human population.

Roving Paragraph Frames

Roving Paragraph Frames is an activity that combines listening, speaking, reading, and writing in an interactive format. Students engage in a series of short conversations, each of which culminates in the creation of a new sentence. The collection of sentences eventually forms a paragraph. This strategy can be used as a warm-up activity, a transition midway through a class period, or as closure to review the day's concepts and learning.

1. To begin the activity, give your students a sentence stem to be completed in writing. Sample: "When describing Abstract Expressionism, it is important to remember_____."

2. Give students a set time to think about the stem and write out their complete sentences.

3. Ask the students to stand up with their paper and pencils when they have completed the written sentence.

4. Have the students "rove" around the room and find a partner.

5. Ask students to read their writing to one another. The first person reads their complete sentence (stem + response). The second person listens and then reads their own complete sentence.

6. The partners then collaborate to write a new sentence that begins with a new stem, such as "*In addition, _____.*" They can either "borrow or steal" each other's responses if they are different, or they can create a fresh sentence.

7. Once sentence number two is complete, partners raise their hands or stand back to back. The key here is to incorporate total response signals to indicate to the teacher that the task is complete. Now they are ready to rove again!

8. Have the students find new partners and repeat the entire process with the second partner. *It is crucial to instruct students to take turns reading everything they have written so far and listening to each other's sentences.* This validates student responses and encourages the use of listening and speaking skills.

9. After reading their first two sentences to each other, students collaborate to write a third sentence with the stem "*Also, ____.*"

10. To conclude, have students repeat the process one last time, roving to find their final partners. Once each partner reads his or her sentences aloud, ask students to write the final sentence using the last stem "*Finally, ____.*" At this point, each student should have a well-constructed paragraph in hand, with transitions and complete thoughts.

Slide Show

Description:

Students prepare a series of scenes in small groups depicting a sequence of events, processes, or procedures.

Directions:

Each group prepares a series of tableaux. A tableaux is a scene where the students serve as silent, motionless characters who are frozen in place to represent a scene from a story in history or a sequence of scenes. The students remain silent and motionless before changing to the next tableaux. Facial expressions, body stance, positioning, and minimal props support each scene. One or two students should serve as narrators to describe the events, processes, or procedures for the audience.

In a social studies class, students portray pivotal scenes of the suffragette era beginning with the 1848 Seneca Falls Convention and ending with the 19th amendment that grants women the right to vote.

In a science class, students portray the Krebs cycle by having each student take the part of a particular enzyme, coenzyme, ATP, or ADP to represent the process.

After watching each presentation, the class reads the passage that was used for the slide show preparation. They then discuss the various ways the group portrayed important ideas from the passage.

SENTENCE STEMS

» They demonstrated __ by...
» They showed how...
» They represented the reasons why...
» I think they were trying to show...

Supported Interview

(adapted from Wilhelm, 2012)

Description:

Students take on the role of historical or fictional characters who have made decisions in history or in literature. The decision-making process becomes evident as they verbalize their thoughts.

Directions:

Begin by choosing one historical or fictional character who has made a significant decision during the course of events in history or literature. Have students brainstorm a list of reasons they think contributed to the character's decision. Then have students list as much information as possible about the character's life using information from textbooks, notes, or other available resources.

Choose a student to play the role of the historical/fictional character. Next, choose three students to act as a visual representation of the character's "mind's eye." Have the main character sit in the front of the classroom with the three other students behind him/her. The student playing the character can ask questions to the "mind's eye" at any time during the interview. Additionally, the students playing the mind's eye can stop the interview and talk with the character at any time.

The rest of the class is the audience and represents other characters from history/literature: reporters, congressmen, townspeople, etc. The audience will take on a role as they interview the character who sits in front of the classroom. For example, a press corp questioning the president, members of Parliament questioning Henry VIII, or the Montagues and Capulets debating with Prince Escalus on how to resolve the conflict between their families. The audience, in their role, may only react to what they hear the character say directly to them. They cannot react to anything said by the mind's eye.

Students taking part in the audience or posing as characters can use these sentence stems:

SENTENCE STEMS

Audience Question Stems	Character Response Stems	Mind's Eye Stems
» My question is...	» Allow me a moment to respond to...	» What you should do is...
» What's your view of...	» My opinion is...	» You might want to think about...
» Can you explain why...	» In response to your question, I think...	
» Clarify your position on...		

Talk Show

Students participate in a talk show where they represent the views of various scientific/historical/literary characters.

Choose a topic for a series of talk shows that students can perform in groups. For example, if studying the causes of global migration in social studies, students can choose from "Life in North Africa and Europe," "Perils of the Mediterranean Journey," "The Rights of Migrants," and "To Migrate or Not to Migrate?" A biology class might choose from these topics: "To Evolve or Not to Evolve: Single Celled Organisms Debate Their Future" or "Global Warming: Time for Decision."

In a chemistry class, students might act as protons, neutrons, or electrons to debate which subatomic particles are most important to the atom. They might each choose an element from the Periodic Table and present why they should be considered for the "Element of the Year" prize, or they might adopt the personas of Niels Bohr, J.J. Thomson, Ernest Rutherford, Democritus, John Dalton, and Erwin Schrödinger to discuss what they believe an atom really looks like.

In small groups, students can prepare an improvised talk show about their topic. They must choose a host, identify characters, prepare questions to ask, and write possible responses. The group can choose to allow audience questions if they wish. Students are encouraged to use humor and surprise but to avoid anachronisms.

SENTENCE STEMS

For Host

» Ladies and Gentlemen, welcome to...

» Our topic today is...

» We have __ with us...

» Now, for our first question...

» The last question for our guest is...

T-Chart, Pair, Defend

Students work in pairs to take on the roles of two characters in conversation about a decision that needs to be made. Characters could be policy makers or scientists, historical figures, or characters from a novel or short story.

This structured conversation allows students to approach a content concept from two opposing viewpoints.

1. Choose a text that will enable students to have a vocabulary-rich conversation from two different points of view.

2. Select a pair of characters related to the text who could have two different points of view.

3. Have students read and annotate the text.

4. Have students brainstorm possible attitudes and beliefs of the two selected characters from the text on a T-chart.

5. Have students form pairs and take turns role-playing the two characters in conversation. Characters could be scientists making a decision, lawmakers debating a bill, or characters from a novel or short story. The conversation always begins with a structured sentence frame.

6. Extension: Select volunteers to perform their dialogues in front of the class and then follow with a class discussion.

The Library of Congress @ Flickr Commons

Here are some samples of possible topics and sentence starters:

Subject	Topic	Sentence Starters	
		A	B
Social Studies	Crusades	We should leave England for the Holy Land because...	We should stay in England because...
Science	The Use of Ethanol for Energy	We must convert America to an ethanol-based economy because...	We should not convert America to an ethanol-based economy because...
Language Arts	The Three Little Pigs	The wolf should blow all the houses down because...	The wolf should not blow all the houses down because...
Math	Setting Up Word Problems	We should set up a table and make a sketch before setting up these equations because...	We should not set up a table and make a sketch before setting up these equations because...
Art	Drawing With Perspective	It's easy to draw with perspective because...	It's difficult to draw with perspective because...

T-Chart, Pair, Defend Continued

The following is a detailed example of two opposing stems with possible student responses:

Harriet Tubman should **escape** because...	Harriet Tubman should not **escape** because...
she knows the outdoors well and has good survival skills.	she could be killed if she is caught by slave catchers.
she has befriended a Quaker woman who lives nearby, and she can help her get to the next station on the UGRR.	her husband, John, refuses to leave and she should remain with her husband.
it is less than 90 miles to the Pennsylvania state line and Philadelphia.	it is just too risky to try to escape alone.
if she is sold southbound, she may never have the chance to escape again.	if she escapes, others might be punished in her place.
if she is successful, she might be able to help others escape also.	slave catchers are everywhere, and there will be a bounty for her capture and return.
her cleverness will help her elude the slave catchers.	her narcolepsy (sleeping spells) increases her chances of being captured.

Vocabulary Art Show

Description:

Students become artists as they reveal the meanings and significance of words.

Directions:

The teacher provides vocabulary terms and definitions to groups of students. In groups, students take on the role of artists who create a visual representation of the vocabulary term. Students can create an abstract or realistic sketch or a sculpture using objects in the room. Students will select one or two representatives to be speakers who explain the visual that they created.

When all the groups have finished, students can take turns interviewing other groups about their works of art using the following stems:

SENTENCE STEMS

for Interview Questions

» What was your term?
» Why did you represent it this way?
» I noticed how you...
» I wondered why you...
» Why did you decide to...

for Responses

» My term was...
» I represented it this way because...
» I did this because....
» I decided that because...

Writing Windows

In this activity, students are presented with an image that they are going to describe in detail. After students generate a list of words to describe the image, they write a paragraph as if they were actually "inside" the image.

In groups of four, students receive different images related to a similar topic. Each image is posted in a folder, one per folder. Students do not reveal their images to each other. In addition, students receive a 5" x 8" lined index card. All students use their index cards to respond to the following instructions:

1. List everything you see in your image.

2. List adjectives that would describe the objects in the image.

3. Use verbs to identify the action you see in your image.

4. Put your pencils down; close your eyes; step into the image and look all around. Now, open your eyes.

The teacher then says, "Now, what else do you see? List what you hear. List what you smell. List what the people are wearing and saying. Put your pencils down."

Provide each student with a second 5" x 8" lined index card featuring a prepared sentence frame prompting the student to write from a perspective within the image. For example, the four sentence stems listed above could be used with four different images of Mission San Jose. After students complete their compositions, they share their writing within their groups and then reveal the image that inspired their writing.

WATCH
Fortify Output
with Writing
Windows

SENTENCE STEMS

» Only a few months ago, we were a nomadic band of people, and now I...

» On Sunday afternoon we hired a chauffeur and motored out to see the ruins of old Mission San Jose, and I...

» There I stood, among the ruins of old Mission San Jose, ready to restore this edifice back to its majestic beauty, and I...

» I slipped away from the tour group and rounded a corner near the old convent to witness the most glorious sight, and I...

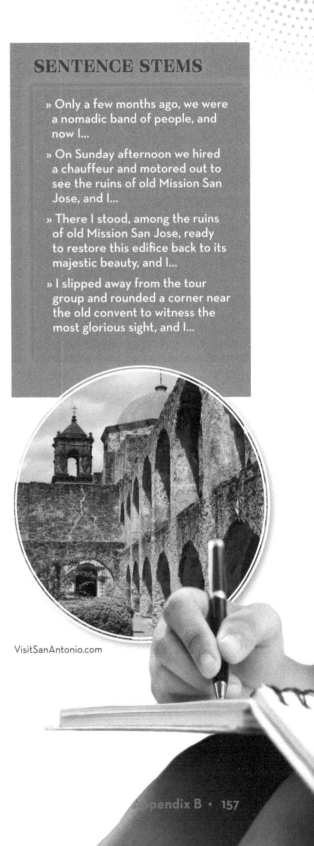

VisitSanAntonio.com

Written Conversation

This activity is a quick writing task designed to practice using content-specific vocabulary from two different perspectives. Pairs of students can engage in Written Conversation in the middle or at the end of a unit of study.

Directions:

After reading a passage or studying a phenomenon or problem, students brainstorm, as a class, the attitudes and beliefs of two characters or objects. Ask students to imagine what one thing, character, or object might say to the other if given a chance.

Students pair up as partner A and partner B. For example, in a social studies class, partner A might be Martin Luther King Jr., and partner B might be Malcom X. Partner

A then begins by writing a short note to partner B. Forms of communication may include texting, letter writing, or in-person conversation. Partner B then reads the note (text/letter/conversation script), writes a response on the same paper, and passes it back. This continues for ten minutes. After that time, the students discuss the note, first with each other, then with the whole class. They may read their dialogues to other groups or out loud to the class.

In a math class, students pass a note representing the views of two characters in a word problem or two different opinions on how to solve a problem.

In a science class, students take on the roles of various objects such as wind and rocks. As they do so, they discuss erosion, E. coli, or host bacteriophage.

SENTENCE STEMS

for Brainstorm

» (Character/Object) probably believes...

» (Character/Object) might say...

» One word/phrase (Character/Object) might say is...

for Notes

» Dear __, I'm writing to express my opinion about...

» You might want to consider the fact that...

» I must respectfully disagree with your thoughts about...

» I see we agree about...

Rules for Written Conversation

a. Each person writes one complete sentence each time the note is passed.

b. Sentences must have capital letters and correct punctuation.

c. Students are to use as many words as they can from the vocabulary brainstorm list or the word wall, and these words must be circled when the activity is concluded.

Yes Conscience/No Conscience

Description:

Students have the opportunity to give advice to a historical or fictional character.

Directions:

Choose a significant decision a historical or fictional character had to make. For example, during the Civil War, William Lloyd Garrison decided to support the Union war effort despite his pacifist beliefs, and in literature, Peeta decides to confess his feelings to Katniss in Hunger Games. As a class, think about the decisions and brainstorm reasons why the person should or should not have made the decision.

Then, have students form groups of three. One student in the group will take on the role of the character; the other two students will take on the role of the person's conscience. One student will try to persuade the character to make a certain decision; the other student will try to persuade the character to make the opposite decision. For example, one student will try to convince William Lloyd Garrison to support the Union war effort, and the other will try to convince him to oppose it.

The character making the decision can speak to the other two students while they verbalize the pros and cons. After five minutes of dialogue, the character must make a decision and state the reasons for the decision. The discussions may be repeated in front of the class.

SENTENCE STEMS

Supporting (YES)

- You should...
- It would be wise to...
- Go ahead and...

Opposing (NO)

- You shouldn't...
- It wouldn't be good to...
- The consequences of...

Character

- I've made my decision. I've chosen to ... because...
- I've decided to...

(Unit Of Study)
Windows On History

Students examine historical images, speak and write from multiple perspectives, and share their writing in order to gain deeper understanding of a broad content concept or topic.

1. Select an image of a historical event to display on a slide.

2. Choose an image of a historical individual/character involved in the event.

3. Select and prepare a text about the event and historical figure.

4. Reproduce the History Scene Investigation (HSI)/Uncover the Picture Template (see below) for each student.

5. Copy the T-Chart (see step 7 on p. 162) with sentence stems for students.

6. Provide a chart with transition words located in step 7 (p. 162) for students.

Outlined below are the detailed steps to conducting a successful Windows on History:

1 **History Scene Investigation (HSI)/ Uncover the Picture**

- Select an image of a historical event to display on a slide. Cover the entire selected image with tiles or text boxes that can be removed during the activity.

- Uncover small portions of the image a little at a time. As the image is slowly revealed, have students list what they see (nouns) using the HSI Uncover the Picture Template (see below).

- Give students three opportunities during this step to predict what the image might be. Ask, "What do you think this is?" "Why do you think that?"

- Finally, reveal the entire image.

HSI – Historical Scene Investigation/Uncover the Picture Data Collection Sheet – Uncover the Picture Template	
The Evidence	**The Predictions**
What do you see? List • • • •	What do you think this is? **First Prediction** I think... **Second Prediction** Now I think... **Third Prediction** I think...

2 Brainstorm Feeling Words (Optional)

- Ask students to view the entire image carefully and list "feeling" words it evokes. "What feeling words come to mind when you view this image?" This can be done individually followed by a share out or as a whole group.

- Record the feeling words on chart paper.

3 Tell Students What the HSI Image Represents

4 Read Text Regarding the HSI Content/Topic of the Image

- Provide students with a short text to read regarding the topic represented in the historical scene.

- Prior to reading, have students use the Scanning technique (Step 5, p. 58) for pre-teaching vocabulary.

- Next, set a purpose for reading the text (e.g., read to answer these questions: Approximately when did the Underground Railroad begin? What were some code terms used on the Underground Railroad?).

- After students silently read the text, discuss answers to the questions with students.

5 The Portrait Character Image

- Present an image of a historical figure closely related to the HSI scene in step 1. Tell students they will be learning more about this individual in a reading passage, text, or story.

6 The Emotional Connection

Scan and Read Text or Have Students Listen to a Story about the Portrait Character

- Have students scan the text from the bottom to the top to find unfamiliar words.

- Record the scanned words on chart paper.

- Quickly define each term to facilitate student comprehension.

- Set a purpose for reading the story using the list of questions from step 4.

- Have students read the text about the historical figure silently.

  OR

- Present the questions from step 4 prior to telling/reading the story.

- Use PowerPoint slides and visuals to tell/read the story of the Portrait Character to students.

- After the story is told/read, have students pair up and discuss their answers to the questions from step 4.

- Have students work in teams to list on chart paper as many facts and details about the Portrait Character as they can within five minutes.

7 Speaker/Leader Discussion: T-Chart, Pair, Defend

- Prepare a T-Chart and brainstorm two perspectives about the historical figure or portrait character and a pivotal decision he/she had to make. For example:

Harriet Tubman should run away because...	Harriet Tubman should not run away because...

- Discuss possible arguments the historical figure must use to make a decision, and record them on the T-Chart.

- Divide students into pairs. Within the pairs, student A is the speaker, and student B is the leader.

- Explain the procedure for the discussion.

Procedure:

1. The speaker begins by defending one point of view using the sentence stem at the top of the T-Chart. For example, "Harriet Tubman should run away because she is only 90 miles from the border."

2. The leader claps once at the end of a speaker's sentence to signal the speaker to use a transition word and switch to the opposite point of view. For example, "On the other hand, Harriet Tubman should not run away because she has narcolepsy, which may increase her chances of getting caught."

3. The leader claps once after the second statement is given. This clap is an effective way to signal to the students that it is time to shift points of view and glance at the Transition Words chart (adapted from Zwiers, 2008). Doing so signals to the speaker to select a transition word and give one statement regarding the other point of view (e.g., "Nevertheless, Harriet should run away because she knows a Quaker woman nearby who could help her.").

Transition Words

However,
On the other hand,
On the contrary,
Yet,
Nevertheless,

4. The leader may clap up to three times during a round.

5. The speaker/leader roles switch after one minute.

6. Repeat Steps one through four.

Note: It is helpful to emphasize to the students that the speaker has to begin their discussion in support of a point-of-view using the sentence stem at the top of the T-Chart. Encourage speakers to include at least three scanned words in their argument.

8 Analyze the HSI Image

- Refer students to the HSI image in step 1. Give each student a large index card.

- Ask students to imagine stepping into the image and make lists after reading the prompts on the following page. Tell students they can use words or phrases to create their lists. Read one prompt at a time in the sequence listed on the following page, leaving about one to two minutes between each prompt.

- List all adjectives that describe the nouns in this image.

- List all the action (ing) verbs you can find in this image.

- What do you smell? Write the list of things down.

- What do you hear? Write the list of things down.

- What are the people wearing? Write the list of things down.

- What are the people saying? Write the words and phrases down.

9 Write and Share a Historical Narrative/Story Using a Sentence Stem

• Given a choice of at least two sentence stems, students will choose one stem representing one point of view to begin their story. For example, "Cold, wet, and shaken, we stumbled through the night until..."

• Students must include at least three scanned words in their writing. *Provide 7 to 10 minutes for students to write in complete silence.

• Have students share their writing with a partner when finished.

10 Change the Point of View for a Historical Narrative (optional)

• Ask students to return to their writing and rewrite it using the third-person point of view. This adds a different perspective to the historical narrative.

11 Write a Letter

• Have students write a letter to the historical figure including the following four elements:

1. Tell a little about yourself.

2. Tell the historical figure/portrait character what qualities you admire about them.

3. Ask for additional information about them.

4. Tell them what you have in common.

12 Share Letters

• Have students share their letters in pairs, groups, or with the entire class.

AFTERWORD

I first learned of Seidlitz Education while attending the seventh International Conference on Immersion and Dual Language Education in North Carolina. The teachers I was working with at the time came to me raving about a session they had just attended with Dr. Mónica Lara, which had included a discussion of *7 Steps to a Language-Rich, Interactive Classroom*. For years, my career as a researcher had been dedicated to promoting programs that enrich education for students facing linguistic hurdles, and I was thrilled to see the teachers so excited. I decided to seek out Dr. Lara and find out about these "7 Steps." When Dr. Lara and I met and she learned about my extensive work as a researcher in the field of language acquisition, she wanted to introduce me to John Seidlitz–the founder of Seidlitz Education. He was in the process of putting together a research team to help investigate the efficacy of the 7 Steps. I came to learn that the team at Seidlitz Education had developed and trained teachers in the 7 Steps methodology across Texas and the United States, and that they had recently branched out into other countries as well.

A variety of programs for teaching multilingual learners have been well researched over many years, including ESL, bilingual education, sheltered instruction, co-teaching models, and many more. Dual-language education has become one of the most successful methods used in U.S. schools to promote academic success for multilingual learners, yet its implementation can be challenging, and it requires a long-term commitment to see it through to fruition. What I believe we need to consider is that a large majority of schools still struggle with finding a successful model of instruction within each language program. The schools I work with are always looking for a set of strategies teachers can easily understand and implement that address the unique needs of the linguistically diverse students in their classrooms. After talking with Dr. Lara, I began to wonder if the straightforward approach of *7 Steps to a Language-Rich, Interactive Classroom* truly might be exactly what these schools are looking for.

I recall my first teaching job in a fourth- and fifth-grade multi-age classroom of 32 students–a somewhat daunting task for a new teacher. I remember being told several students were not fluent in English. What wasn't mentioned was that the students spoke eight different native languages and were at vastly different levels of English proficiency! We, of course, only had English-language resources at that time, which made it even more challenging to meet the academic needs of multilingual learners. What I desperately needed was a guide to show me how I could successfully teach students who came from diverse language backgrounds. Perhaps knowing about the 7 Steps back then would have made a difference!

Talking with the team at Seidlitz Education made me believe that *7 Steps to a Language-Rich, Interactive Classroom* might offer an instructional delivery model that actually addresses these issues. Reflecting upon my years of experience with a multitude of approaches to teaching multilingual learners, I was filled with great interest to learn more about the potential of this methodology. It seemed to offer easy-to-implement

> *"I have come to understand that developing the 7 Steps in schools requires that educators at many levels are involved in the process for the program to reach its full potential..."*
>
> – Sharon R. Goldman, CITA Education

solutions for teachers of the diverse student populations at all levels, promoting engagement and improving proficiency for all learners–not just English learners. After much consideration, I agreed to coordinate the Seidlitz Education research team.

John Seidlitz spearheaded the research initiative with his talented colleagues, and coordinating *The 7 Steps Study* protocol with this team has afforded me the opportunity to understand the core components of the program. Together we developed a longitudinal study of 7 Steps pedagogy at the middle school level to evaluate data from years of implementation across the state of Texas. After completing hundreds of observations of 7 Steps classroom implementation, we now know how well it really works. I have witnessed students being given a voice to share what they know and taking risks with their emerging language skills. Teachers who have developed a 7 Steps system that differentiates for all of their students are the most successful at authentically engaging multilingual students in the process of learning at very high levels. And the best part is how practical and streamlined this methodology is to develop in their classrooms.

I have come to understand that developing the 7 Steps in schools requires that educators at many levels are involved in the process for the program to reach its full potential–teachers, instructional coaches, professional development specialists, administrators, curriculum specialists, and researchers all have parts to play. Start by implementing the 7 Steps, then take it a little further with the activities, and when you see the students growing and engaging through their own initiative, use the "Step It Up" recommendations to further develop their independence, their tool kits, and their higher-order thinking!

As you implement the practices you find in this book, please share with us any thoughts, questions, or insights you have. *The 7 Steps Study* is currently in the second phase of its three-phase research model. We hope to gain extensive knowledge regarding program effectiveness as this research progresses, and we anticipate finding even more evidence to support its wide use in traditional and dual-language classrooms around the world.

– Sharon R. Goldman, CITA Education

BIBLIOGRAPHY

Aguirre-Muñoz, Z. (2011). Helping ELs reason mathematically through explicit language moves: towards meaningful participation. *AccELLerate!*, 10.

Allington, R. L. (2002). What I've learned about effective reading instruction: From a decade of studying exemplary elementary classroom teachers. *Phi Delta Kappan*, *83*(10), 740-747.

Anderson, L. W., & Bloom, B. S. (2001). *A taxonomy for learning, teaching, and assessing: A revision of Bloom's taxonomy of educational objectives*. Longman.

Asher, J. J., & Price, B. S. (1967). The learning strategy of the total physical response: Some age differences. *Child Development*, 1219-1227.

August, D. E., & Shanahan, T. E. (2006). *Developing literacy in second-language learners: Report of the National Literacy Panel on Language-Minority Children and Youth*. Lawrence Erlbaum Associates Publishers.

Bai, Z. (2018). An analysis of English vocabulary learning strategies. *Journal of language Teaching and Research*, *9*(4), 849-855.

Bailey, A. L., & Carroll, P. E. (2015). Assessment of English language learners in the era of new academic content standards. *Review of Research in Education*, *39*(1), 253-294.

Baker, S., Lesaux, N., Jayanthi, M., Dimino, J., Proctor, C.P., Morris, J., Gersten, R., Haymond, K., Kieffer, M.J., Linan-Thompson, S. and Newman-Gonchar, R., (2014). Teaching academic content and literacy to English learners in elementary and middle school. *IES Practice Guide*. NCEE 2014-4012. IES.

Baker, W., & Boonkit, K. (2004). Learning strategies in reading and writing: EAP contexts. *RELC Journal*, *35*(3), 299-328.

Bakr, S. M. (2004). *The efficacy of some proposed activities for developing creative thinking of English learners at the preparatory stage (Second Year)* (ED502827). ERIC. https://files.eric.ed.gov/fulltext/ED502827.pdf

Barrow, L., & Markman-Pithers, L. (2016). Supporting young English learners in the United States. *The Future of Children*, *26*(2), 159-183.

Baumann, J. F., Jones, L. A., & Seifert-Kessell, N. (1993). Using think alouds to enhance children's comprehension monitoring abilities. *The Reading Teacher*, *47*(3), 184-193.

Beck, I. L., McKeown, M. G., & Kucan, L. (2013). *Bringing words to life: Robust vocabulary instruction*. Guilford Press.

Berg, E. C. (1999). The effects of trained peer response on ESL students' revision types and writing quality. *Journal of Second Language Writing*, *8*(3), 215-241.

Bickel, W.E., & Bickel, D.D. (1986). Effective schools, classrooms, and instruction: Implications for special education. *Exceptional Children*, 52(6) 489-500.

Birgili, B. (2015). Creative and critical thinking skills in problem-based learning environments. *Journal of Gifted Education and Creativity*, *2*(2), 71-80.

Boekaerts, M., Zeidner, M., & Pintrich, P. R. (Eds.). (2000). *Handbook of self-regulation*. Academic Press.

Boulware, B. J., & Crow, M. L. (2008). Using the concept attainment strategy to enhance reading comprehension. *The Reading Teacher*, *61*(6), 491-495.

Brandes, D. R., & McMaster, K. L. (2017). A review of morphological analysis strategies on vocabulary outcomes with ELLs. *Insights into Learning Disabilities*, *14*(1), 53-72.

Brooks, S., Dobbins, K., Scott, J. J., Rawlinson, M., & Norman, R. I. (2014). Learning about learning outcomes: the student perspective. *Teaching in Higher Education*, *19*(6), 721-733.

Brown, A. L., Campione, J. C., & Day, J. D. (1981). Learning to learn: On training students to learn from texts. *Educational Researcher*, *10*(2), 14-21.

Bruner, J. S. (1973). Organization of early skilled action. *Child Development*, 1-11.

Kalnins, I. V., & Bruner, J. S. (1973). The coordination of visual observation and instrumental behavior in early infancy. *Perception*, *2*(3), 307-314.

Cakmakci, G., Aydeniz, M., Brown, A., & Makokha, J. M. (2020). Situated cognition and cognitive apprenticeship learning. In Akpan, B., & Kennedy, T. J. (Eds.). *Science education in theory and practice: An introductory guide to learning theory*. (pp. 293-310). Springer Nature.

Calderón, M., Slavin, R., & Sanchez, M. (2011). Effective instruction for English learners. *The Future of Children*, 103-127.

Calderón, M. E., & Minaya-Rowe, L. (2010). *Preventing long-term ELs: Transforming schools to meet core standards*. Corwin Press.

Calderón, M. E., & Slakk, S. (2018). *Teaching reading to English learners, grades 6-12: A framework for improving achievement in the content areas*. Corwin Press.

Caldwell, J. E. (2007). Clickers in the large classroom: Current research and best-practice tips. *CBE—Life Sciences Education*, *6*(1), 9-20.

Callow, J. (2008). Show me: Principles for assessing students' visual literacy. *The Reading Teacher*, *61*(8), 616-626.

Cavanaugh, R. A., Heward, W. L., & Donelson, F. (1996). Effects of response cards during lesson closure on the academic performance of secondary students in an earth science course. *Journal of Applied Behavior Analysis*, *29*(3), 403-406.

Celce-Murcia, M., Brinton, D. M., & Goodwin, J. M. (Eds.). (1996). *Teaching pronunciation: A reference for teachers of English to speakers of other languages*. Cambridge University Press.

Chadha, A. (2019). Deepening engagement: The intimate flow of online interactions. *International Journal of Online Pedagogy and Course Design (IJOPCD)*, *9*(3), 32-47.

Chamot, A. U. (2005). Language learning strategy instruction: Current issues and research. *Annual Review of Applied Linguistics*, *25*, 112-130.

Chamot, A. U., & O'Malley, J. M. (1996). The cognitive academic language learning approach: A model for linguistically diverse classrooms. *The Elementary School Journal, 96*(3), 259-273.

Cheung, A. C., & Slavin, R. E. (2012). Effective reading programs for Spanish-dominant English language learners (ELLs) in the elementary grades: A synthesis of research. *Review of Educational Research, 82*(4), 351-395.

Chohan, S. K. (2010). Whispering selves and reflective transformations in the internal dialogue of teachers and students. *Journal of Invitational Theory and Practice, 16*, 10-29.

Christenson, S. L., Reschly, A. L., & Wylie, C. (Eds.). (2012). *Handbook of research on student engagement.* Springer Science & Business Media.

Christle, C. A., & Schuster, J. W. (2003). The effects of using response cards on student participation, academic achievement, and on-task behavior during whole-class, math instruction. *Journal of Behavioral Education, 12*(3), 147-165.

Clay, M. M. (1991). *Becoming literate: The construction of inner control.* Heinemann.

Cross, J. (2010). Raising L2 listeners' metacognitive awareness: A sociocultural theory perspective. *Language Awareness, 19*(4), 281-297.

Cross, J. (2011). Metacognitive instruction for helping less-skilled listeners. *ELT journal, 65*(4), 408-416.

Crowell, A., & Kuhn, D. (2014). Developing dialogic argumentation skills: A 3-year intervention study. *Journal of Cognition and Development, 15*(2), 363-381.

Cummins, J. (2007). Rethinking monolingual instructional strategies in multilingual classrooms. *Canadian Journal of Applied Linguistics, 10*(2), 221-240.

Daniels, H., & Steineke, N. (2004). *Mini-lessons for literature circles.* Heinemann.

de Araujo, Z., Roberts, S. A., Willey, C., & Zahner, W. (2018). English learners in K–12 mathematics education: A review of the literature. *Review of Educational Research, 88*(6), 879-919.

De Smedt, F., & Van Keer, H. (2018). Fostering writing in upper primary grades: A study into the distinct and combined impact of explicit instruction and peer assistance. *Reading and Writing, 31*(2), 325-354.

Diamond, L., & Gutlohn, L. (2006). *Vocabulary handbook.* Brookes.

Didion, L. A., Toste, J. R., & Wehby, J. H. (2020). Response cards to increase engagement and active participation of middle school students with EBD. *Remedial and Special Education, 41*(2), 111-123.

Dole, J. A., Duffy, G. G., Roehler, L. R., & Pearson, P. D. (1991). Moving from the old to the new: Research on reading comprehension instruction. *Review of Educational Research, 61*(2), 239-264.

Donnelly, W. B., & Roe, C. J. (2010). Using sentence frames to develop academic vocabulary for English learners. *The Reading Teacher, 64*(2), 131-136.

Duffy, G. G. (2002). The case for direct explanation of strategies. In C.C. Block & M. Pressley (Eds.) *Comprehension instruction: Research-based best practices*, 28-41. Guilford Press.

Dutro, S., & Moran, C. (2003). Rethinking English language instruction: An architectural approach. In G. G. García (Ed.), *English learners: Reaching the highest level of English literacy* (pp. 227–258). International Reading Association.

Dutro, S., & Smith, D. (2015). Lines of Communication. In *Cue Cards: Routines for Student Interaction*. E.L. Achieve.

Echevarria, J., Vogt, M., & Short, D. (2017). *Making content comprehensible for English learners: The SIOP model (5th ed.)*. Pearson.

Elbow, P. (1998). *Writing without teachers*. Oxford University Press.

Ennis, R. H. (1987). A taxonomy of critical thinking dispositions and abilities. In J. B. Baron & R. J. Sternberg (Eds.), *Series of books in psychology. Teaching thinking skills: Theory and practice* (p. 9–26). W H Freeman/Times Books/ Henry Holt & Co.

Eyraud, K., Giles, G., Koenig, S., & Stoller, F.L. (2000). The word wall approach: Promoting L2 vocabulary learning. *English Teaching Forum*, 38(3), 2-11.

Facione, P. A., & Facione, N. C. (1994). Holistic critical thinking scoring rubric. The California Academic Press/Insight Assessment.

Fisher, D., & Frey, N. (2007). Implementing a schoolwide literacy framework: Improving achievement in an urban elementary school. *The Reading Teacher, 61*(1), 32-43.

Fisher, D., Frey, N., Fearn, L., Farnan, N., & Petersen, F. (2004). Increasing writing achievement in an urban middle school. *Middle School Journal*, 36(2), 21-26.

Florez, M. C. (1998). *Improving adult ESL learners' pronunciation skills* (ED427553). ERIC. https://files.eric. ed.gov/fulltext/ED427553.pdf

Foundation for Critical Thinking. (2019, n.d.). *Defining critical thinking.* https://www.criticalthinking.org/pages/ defining-critical-thinking/766.

Fountas, I. C., & Pinnell, G. S. (2001). *Guiding readers and writers, grades 3-6: Teaching comprehension, genre, and content literacy*. Heinemann.

Freeman-Green, S., Driver, M. K., Wang, P., Kamuru, J., & Jackson, D. (2021). Culturally sustaining practices in content area instruction for CLD students with learning disabilities. *Learning Disabilities Research & Practice, 36*(1), 12-25.

Ganapathy, M., & Kaur, S. (2014). ESL students' perceptions of the use of higher order thinking skills in English language writing. *Advances in Language and Literary Studies, 5*(5), 80-87.

García, O. (2014). US Spanish and education: Global and local intersections. *Review of Research in Education*, 38(1), 58-80.

Gardner III, R., Heward, W. L., & Grossi, T. A. (1994). Effects of response cards on student participation and academic achievement: A systematic replication with inner-city students during whole-class science instruction. *Journal of Applied Behavior Analysis*, 27(1), 63-71.

Gearing, N. V., & Hart, L. C. (2019). The impact of adding written discourse to six year olds' mathematics explanations within a problem-based learning unit. *European Journal of STEM Education*, 4(1), 3.

Geva, E. (2006). Second-language oral proficiency and second-language literacy. In August, D. E., & Shanahan, T. E. (Eds.) *Developing literacy in second-language learners: Report of the National Literacy Panel on Language-Minority Children and Youth*, 123-139. Lawrence Erlbaum Associates Publishers.

Gibbons, P. (2002). *Scaffolding language, scaffolding learning: Teaching second language learners in the mainstream classroom*. Heinemann.

Gibbons, P. (2015). *Scaffolding language, scaffolding learning: Teaching second language learners in the mainstream classroom*. Heinemann.

Goh, C. C. (2014). Reconceptualising second language oracy instruction: Metacognitive engagement and direct teaching in listening and speaking. *AJELP: Asian Journal of English Language and Pedagogy*, 2, 1-20.

Goldenberg, C. (1992). Instructional conversations: Promoting comprehension through discussion. *The Reading Teacher*, 46(4), 316-326.

Goldenberg, C. (2013). Unlocking the research on English learners: What we know--and don't yet know--about effective instruction. *American Educator*, 37(2), 4.

Goldman, S. R., Seidlitz, J., Lara, M., & Fleenor, S. J. (2021). The 7 steps study: Evaluating program effectiveness for teaching English learners. American Education Research Association: Online Repository. https://www.aera.net/Publications/Online-Paper-Repository/AERA-Online-Paper-Repository/7-Steps-Study

Graff, G. (2008). *Clueless in academe: How schooling obscures the life of the mind*. Yale University Press.

Graham, S., Kiuhara, S. A., & MacKay, M. (2020). The effects of writing on learning in science, social studies, and mathematics: A meta-analysis. *Review of Educational Research*, 90(2), 179-226.

Graham, S., Liu, X., Bartlett, B., Ng, C., Harris, K. R., Aitken, A., Barkel, A., Kavanaugh, C., & Talukdar, J. (2018). Reading for writing: A meta-analysis of the impact of reading interventions on writing. *Review of Educational Research*, 88(2), 243-284.

Grapin, S. (2019). Multimodality in the new content standards era: Implications for English learners. *Tesol Quarterly*, 53(1), 30-55.

Gunuc, S. (2014). The relationships between student engagement and their academic achievement. *International Journal on New Trends in Education and their Implications*, 5(4), 216-231.

Gunuc, S., & Kuzu, A. (2015). Student engagement scale: development, reliability and validity. *Assessment & Evaluation in Higher Education*, 40(4), 587-610.

Guthrie, J.T., & Ozgungor, S. (2002). Instructional contexts for reading engagement. In C.C. Block & M. Pressley (Eds.). *Comprehension instruction: Research-based best practices* (pp. 275-288). Guilford Press.

Guzzetti, B. J., Snyder, T. E., Glass, G. V., & Gamas, W. S. (1993). Promoting conceptual change in science: A comparative meta-analysis of instructional interventions from reading education and science education. *Reading Research Quarterly*, 28(2), 117-159.

Harrington, M. J. (1996). Basic instruction in word analysis skills to improve spelling competence. *Education*, 117(1), 22-31.

Hattie, J. (2015). High-impact leadership. *Educational leadership*, 72(5), 36-40.

Haukås, Å., Bjørke, C. & Dypedahl, M. (2018). *Metacognition in language learning and teaching*. Taylor & Francis.

Head, M. H., Readence, J. E., & Buss, R. R. (1989). An examination of summary writing as a measure of reading comprehension. *Literacy Research and Instruction*, 28(4), 1-11.

Hemphill, F. C., & Vanneman, A. (2011). Achievement gaps: How hispanic and white students in public schools perform in mathematics and reading on the National Assessment of Educational Progress. Statistical Analysis Report. NCES 2011-459. *National Center for Education Statistics*.

Hill, J., & Flynn, K. (2006). *Classroom instruction that works with English language learners*. Association for Supervision and Curriculum Development.

Hill, J., & Miller, K. B. (2013). *Classroom instruction that works with English language learners* (2nd Ed.). ASCD.

Hopkins, M., Lowenhaupt, R., & Sweet, T. M. (2015). Organizing English learner instruction in new immigrant destinations: District infrastructure and subject-specific school practice. *American Educational Research Journal*, 52(3), 408-439.

Invernizzi, M., & Hayes, L. (2004). Developmental-spelling research: A systematic imperative. *Reading Research Quarterly*, 39(2), 216-228.

Irby, B., Quiros, A. M., Lara-Alecio, R., Rodriguez, L., & Mathes, P. (2008). What administrators should know about a research-based oral language development intervention for English language learners: A description of story retelling and higher order thinking for English language and literacy acquisition--STELLA. *International Journal of Educational Leadership Preparation*, 3(2), n2.

Irvine, J. (2017). A comparison of revised Bloom and Marzano's new taxonomy of learning. *Research in Higher Education Journal, 33.*

Jacob, S., Nguyen, H., Tofel-Grehl, C., Richardson, D., & Warschauer, M. (2018). Teaching computational thinking to English learners. *NYS TESOL journal, 5*(2).

Jenkins, J. R., Stein, M. L., & Wysocki, K. (1984). Learning vocabulary through reading. *American Educational Research Journal, 21*(4), 767-787.

Jensen, E. (2005). *Teaching with the brain in mind* (2nd Ed.). ASCD.

Jensen Jr, R. D. (2015). The effectiveness of the socratic method in developing critical thinking skills in English language learners. *Online Submission.*

Johnson, D., Johnson, B., & Schlichting, K. (2004). Language play: Essential for literacy. In Kame'enui, E. J., & Baumann, J. F. (Eds.). *Vocabulary instruction: Research to practice* (pp. 210-230). Guilford Press.

Johnson, D.W., & Johnson, R.T. (1999). *Learning together and alone: Cooperative, competitive, and individualistic learning.* Allyn & Bacon.

Johnson, D.W., & Johnson, R. T. (1999). Making cooperative learning work. *Theory into practice, 38*(2), 67-73.

Johnson, D.W., Maruyama, G., Johnson, R., Nelson, D., & Skon, L. (1981). Effects of cooperative, competitive, and individualistic goal structures on achievement: A meta-analysis. *Psychological bulletin, 89*(1), 47-62.

Kabilan, M. K. (2000). Creative and critical thinking in language classrooms. *The Internet TESOL Journal, 6*(6), 1-3.

Kagan, S. (1992). *Cooperative learning.* Kagan Cooperative Learning.

Kagan, S. (1995). We can talk: Cooperative learning in the elementary ESL classroom. *ERIC Digest.*

Kaplan, S. N. (2013). Depth and complexity. In Callahan, C. M., & Hertberg-Davis, H. L. (Eds.). *Fundamentals of gifted education: Considering multiple perspectives.* 277-286. Routledge.

Kibler, K., & Chapman, L. A. (2019). Six tips for using culturally relevant texts in diverse classrooms. *The Reading Teacher, 72*(6), 741-744.

Knight, J. (2008). *Coaching: Approaches and perspectives.* Corwin Press.

Kraft, M. A. (2020). Interpreting effect sizes of education interventions. *Educational Researcher, 49*(4), 241-253.

Krashen, S. (1982). Principles and practice in second language acquisition. 65-78. Pergamon Press Inc.

Kuo, F. R., Hwang, G. J., Chen, S. C., & Chen, S. Y. (2012). A cognitive apprenticeship approach to facilitating web-based collaborative problem solving. *Journal of Educational Technology & Society, 15*(4), 319-331.

Lara-Alecio, R., Tong, F., Irby, B. J., Guerrero, C., Huerta, M., & Fan, Y. (2012). The effect of an instructional intervention on middle school English learners' science and English reading achievement. *Journal of Research in Science Teaching, 49*(8), 987-1011.

Lara, M., & Seidlitz, J. (2013). *Supporting English language learners through ongoing and sustained professional development: A 7 Steps approach.* Canter Press.

Lavery, M. R., Nutta, J., & Youngblood, A. (2019). Analyzing student learning gains to evaluate differentiated teacher preparation for fostering English learners' achievement in linguistically diverse classrooms. *Journal of Teacher Education, 70*(4), 372-387.

LeDoux, J. (1998) *The emotional brain.* Simon and Schuster.

LeDoux, J. E. (1993). Emotional memory systems in the brain. *Behavioural brain research, 58*(1-2), 69-79.

Leeman, J. (2003). Recasts and second language development: Beyond negative evidence. *Studies in second language acquisition,* 25(01), 37-63.

Leith, C., Rose, E., & King, T. (2016). Teaching mathematics and language to English learners. *The Mathematics Teacher, 109*(9), 670-678.

Lesaux, N. K., & Geva, E. (2006). Synthesis: Development of literacy in language-minority students. In D. August & T. Shanahan (Eds.), *Developing literacy in second-language learners: Report of the National Literacy Panel on Language-Minority Children and Youth* (p. 53–74). Lawrence Erlbaum Associates Publishers.

Levine, S. (2019). Using everyday language to support students in constructing thematic interpretations. *Journal of the Learning Sciences, 28*(1), 1-31.

Linda, A., & Shah, P. M. (2020). Vocabulary acquisition style in the ESL classroom: A survey on the use of vocabulary learning strategies by the primary 3 learners. *Creative Education, 11*(10), 1973.

Lipson, M. Y., & Wixson, K. K. (2008). *Assessment and instruction of reading and writing difficulty: An interactive approach* (3rd Ed.). Allyn & Bacon.

Lyman, F. (1987). Think-Pair-Share: An expanding teaching technique. *MAA-CIE Cooperative News* 1(1), 1–2.

Maccini, P., & Gagnon, J. C. (2000). Best practices for teaching mathematics to secondary students with special needs. *Focus on exceptional children, 32*(5).

Macon, J. M., Bewell, D., and Vogt, M. (1991). *Responses to literature.* IRA.

Manzo, A. V. (1969). The request procedure. *Journal of Reading,* 13(2), 123-163.

Marzano, R. J. (2004). *Building background knowledge for academic achievement: Research on what works in schools.* ASCD.

Marzano, R. J., Pickering, D., & Pollock, J. E. (2001). *Classroom instruction that works: Research-based strategies for increasing student achievement.* ASCD.

Mayer, R. E. (2004). Should there be a three-strikes rule against pure discovery learning?. *American psychologist, 59*(1), 14.

McDougall, D., & Cordeiro, P. (1992). Effects of random questioning expectations on education majors' preparedness for lecture and discussion. *College Student Journal, 26*(2), 193-198.

McDougall, D., & Cordeiro, P. (1993). Effects of random questioning expectations on community college students' preparedness for lecture and discussion. *Community College Journal of Research and Practice*, 17, 39-49.

McLaughlin, M. (2003). *Guided comprehension in the primary grades.* International Reading Association.

Meisinger, E. B., Schwanenflugel, P. J., Bradley, B. A., & Stahl, S. A. (2004). Interaction quality during partner reading. *Journal of Literacy Research, 36*(2), 111-140.

Meyen, E., Vergason, G., & Whelan, R. (1996). *Strategies for teaching exceptional children in inclusive settings.* Love Pub Co.

Migration Policy Institute (2018). ELL Information Center. https://www.migrationpolicy.org/programs/migration-data-hub

Miller, B., Vehar, J. R., & Firestein, R. L. (2001). *Creativity unbound: An introduction to creative process* (3rd Ed.). Innovation Resources Inc.

Morita-Mullaney, T. (2018). The intersection of language and race among English learner (EL) leaders in desegregated urban midwest schools: A LangCrit narrative study. *Journal of Language, Identity & Education, 17*(6), 371-387.

Nation's Report Card. (2017). *NAEP mathematics & reading assessments: Highlighted results at Grade 4 and 8 for the nation, states, and district.* U.S. Department of Education and the Institute of Education Sciences (IES), National Center for Educational Statistics. https://www.nationsreportcard.gov/reading_math_2017_highlights/.

Nation's Report Card. (2019). *Data Tools: State Profiles – Texas.* U.S. Department of Education and the Institute of Education Sciences (IES), National Center for Educational Statistics. www.nationsreportcard.gov/profiles/stateprofile/overview/TX

National Center for Educational Statistics. (2019). *The condition of education 2019.* Institute of Education Sciences. https://nces.ed.gov/pubsearch/pubsinfo.asp?pubid=2019144.

National Reading Panel (US), National Institute of Child Health, & Human Development (US). (2000). *Teaching children to read: An evidence-based assessment of the scientific research literature on reading and its implications for reading instruction: Reports of the subgroups.* National Institute of Child Health and Human Development, National Institutes of Health.

National Paideia Center (n.d.). The Paideia Principles. https://www.paideia.org/our-approach/paideia-principles

Nejmaoui, N. (2019). Improving EFL learners' critical thinking skills in argumentative writing. *English Language Teaching, 12*(1), 98-109.

Noe, K. L. S., & Johnson, N. J. (1999). *Getting started with literature circles. The Bill Harp professional teachers library series*. Christopher-Gordon Publishers, Inc.

Novak, J. D. (1995). Concept mapping: A strategy for organizing knowledge. In Glynn, S. M., & Duit, R. (Eds.). *Learning science in the schools: Research reforming practice*. Routledge. 229-245.

Nunan, D. (2015). *Teaching English to speakers of other languages: An introduction*. Routledge.

Nuthall, G., & Alton-Lee, A. (1995). Assessing classroom learning: How students use their knowledge and experience to answer classroom achievement test questions in science and social studies. *American Educational Research Journal*, *32*(1), 185-223.

Office of English Language Acquisition. (2019). *Adolescent and adult English learners: A national profile of educational and employment barriers and opportunities*. U.S. Department of Education.

Ogle, D. M. (1986). KWL: A teaching model that develops active reading of expository text. *The Reading Teacher*, 39(6), 564-570.

Parnes, S. J. (1985). Creative problem solving. In A.L. Costa (Ed.), *Developing minds: A resource book for teaching thinking*, 230-232.

Pauk, W., & Owens, R. J. (2013). *How to study in college*. Cengage Learning.

Perry, J., Lundie, D., & Golder, G. (2019). Metacognition in schools: what does the literature suggest about the effectiveness of teaching metacognition in schools?. *Educational Review*, *71*(4), 483-500.

Pilgreen, J. L. (2000). *The SSR handbook: How to organize and manage a sustained silent reading program*. Boynton/Cook Publishers.

Pimentel, S. (2018). *English Learners and Content-Rich Curricula*. Johns Hopkins Institute for Education Policy.

Portes, P. R., González Canché, M., Boada, D., & Whatley, M. E. (2018). Early evaluation findings from the instructional conversation study: Culturally responsive teaching outcomes for diverse learners in elementary school. *American Educational Research Journal*, *55*(3), 488-531.

Qualtrics. (2013). Version 37,892. Provo, Utah, USA.

R Core Team (2016). A language and environment for statistical computing. R Foundation for Statistical Computing, Vienna, Austria. http://www.R-project.org/

Randolph, J. J. (2007). Meta-analysis of the research on response cards: Effects on test achievement, quiz achievement, participation, and off-task behavior. *Journal of Positive Behavior Interventions*, *9*(2), 113-128.

Razfar, A. (2010). Repair with confianza: Rethinking the context of corrective feedback for English learners (ELs). *English Teaching: Practice and Critique*, *9*(2), 11-31.

Rolle, R. A., & Jimenez-Castellanos, O. (2014). An efficacy analysis of the Texas school funding formula with particular attention to English language learners. *Journal of Education Finance, 39*(3), 203-221.

Rose, M. (1989). *Lives on the boundary.* Viking Penguin.

Rosli, M. F. M., & Maarof, N. (2016). The effects of higher order thinking skills (HOTS) questions in improving ESL pupils' writing performance.

Ruddell, M. R., & Shearer, B. A. (2002). "Extraordinary," "Tremendous," "Exhilarating" "Magnificent": Middle school at-risk students become avid word learners with the vocabulary self-collection strategy (VSS). *Journal of Adolescent & Adult Literacy,* 45(5), 352-363.

Samway, K. D. (2006). *When English language learners write* (Vol. 9). Heinemann.

Santibañez, L., & Gándara, P. (2018). Teachers of English language learners in secondary schools: Gaps in preparation and support. *Civil Rights Project-Proyecto Derechos Civiles.*

Scarcella, R. (2002). Some key factors affecting English learners' development of advanced literacy. In Schleppegrell, M. J., & Colombi, M. C. (Eds.). *Developing advanced literacy in first and second languages: Meaning with power.* Routledge, 209-226.

Schagen, I., & Hodgen, E. (2009). How much difference does it make? Notes on understanding, using, and calculating effect sizes for schools. *Research Division, Ministry of Education and Edith Hodgen, New Zealand Council for Educational Research.*

Schmoker, M. (2006). *Results now: How we can achieve unprecedented improvements in teaching and learning.* ASCD.

Schmoker, M. (2018). *Focus: Elevating the essentials to radically improve student learning.* Ascd.

Schneider, M. K. (2019). *Addressing the needs of middle school English learners through inclusion in general education classrooms: A case study of a Midwestern metropolitan public school district.* [Doctoral Dissertation, University of Nebraska - Lincoln]. DigitalCommons@ University of Nebraska-Lincoln. https://digitalcommons.unl.edu/cehsedaddiss/304/

Seidlitz, J., & Perryman, B. (2008). *Seven steps to building an interactive classroom: Engaging all students in academic conversation.* Seidlitz Education.

Short, D. J. (2017). How to integrate content and language learning effectively for English language learners. *Eurasia Journal of Mathematics, Science and Technology Education, 13*(7b), 4237-4260.

Singh, C. K. S., Singh, R. K. A., Singh, T. S. M., Mostafa, N. A., & Mohtar, T. M. T. (2018). Developing a higher order thinking skills module for weak ESL learners. *English Language Teaching, 11*(7), 86-100.

Slama, R. B. (2012). A longitudinal analysis of academic English proficiency outcomes for adolescent English language learners in the United States. *Journal of Educational Psychology, 104*(2), 265.

Smith, M. W., & Wilhelm, J. D. (2002). *Reading don't fix no Chevys: Literacy in the lives of young men.* Heinemann.

Snow, C. E., Griffin, P. E., & Burns, M. (2005). *Knowledge to support the teaching of reading: Preparing teachers for a changing world.* Jossey-Bass.

Spangenberg-Urbschat, K., & Pritchard, R. (1994). *Kids come in all languages: Reading instruction for ESL students.* International Reading Association.

Stahl, S.A., & Fairbanks, M.M. (1986). The Effects of vocabulary instruction: A model-based meta-analysis. *Review of Educational Research, 56*(1), 72-110. Suárez-Orozco, M., & Suárez-Orozco, C. (2015). Children of immigration. *The Phi Delta Kappan, 97*(4), 8-14.

Sweller, J., Kirschner, P. A., & Clark, R. E. (2007). Why minimally guided teaching techniques do not work: A reply to commentaries. *Educational psychologist, 42*(2), 115-121.

Taba, H. (1967). Teachers' handbook for elementary social studies. *Addison-Wesley Publishing Co., Inc.*

Taylor, W. L. (1953). "Cloze procedure": A new tool for measuring readability. *Journalism quarterly, 30*(4), 415-433.

Teemant, A., Hausman, C.S., & Kigamwa, J.C. (2016). The effects of higher order thinking on student achievement and English proficiency. *INTESOL Journal, 13*(1), pp. 1-22.

Texas Education Agency. (2019) *STAAR Statewide Summary Reports 2018-2019.* https://tea.texas.gov/Student_Testing_and_Accountability/Testing/State_of_Texas_Assessments_of_Academic_Readiness_(STAAR)/STAAR_Statewide_Summary_Reports_2018-2019/

Thornberry, T. P. (2005). Explaining multiple patterns of offending across the life course and across generations. *The Annals of the American Academy of Political and Social Science, 602*(1), 156-195.

Tincani, M., & Twyman, J. S. (2016). Enhancing engagement through active student response. *Center on Innovations in Learning, Temple University.*

Torrance, E. P. (1969). Creativity. What research says to the teacher. Washington, DC: National Education Association.

Torrance, E. P. (1979). *The search for satori & creativity.* Creative Education Foundation.

Torrance, E. P. (2018). *Guiding creative talent.* Pickle Partners Publishing.

Twyman, J. S., & Heward, W. L. (2018). How to improve student learning in every classroom now. *International Journal of Educational Research, 87,* 78-90.

Uba, E., Oteikwu, E. A., Onwuka, E., & Abiodun-Eniayekan, E. (2017). A research-based evidence of the effect of graphic organizers on the understanding of prose fiction in ESL classroom. *SAGE Open, 7*(2).

Vail, N. J., & Papenfuss, J. F. (2000). *Daily oral language: Teacher's manual.* Grade 7. Great Source Education Group.

Vogt, M., & Nagano, P. (2003). Turn it on with light bulb reading! Sound-switching strategies for struggling readers. *The Reading Teacher, 57*(3), 214-221.

Von Esch, K., Motha, S., and Kubota, R. (2020). Race and language teaching. *Language Teaching, 53*(4), 391-421.

Walsh, D., & Paul, R. W. (1986). The goal of critical thinking: From educational ideal to educational reality. *American Federation of Teachers.* https://eric. ed.gov/?id=ED295916

Wang, H. C. (2019). Fostering learner creativity in the English L2 classroom: Application of the creative problem-solving model. *Thinking Skills and Creativity, 31*, 58-69.

Weaver, C. (1996). *Teaching grammar in context.* Boynton/Cook Publishers, Inc.

Weinburgh, M., Silva, C., Malloy, R., Marshall, J., & Smith, K. (2012). Methods & Strategies: A Science Lesson or Language Lesson? *Science and Children, 49*(9), 72-76.

Wennerstrom, A. (2001). *The music of everyday speech: Prosody and discourse analysis.* Oxford University Press.

Wessels, S. (2011). Promoting vocabulary learning for English learners. *The Reading Teacher, 65*(1), 46-50.

White, T. G., Sowell, J., & Yanagihara, A. (1989). Teaching elementary students to use word-part clues. *The Reading Teacher, 42*(4), 302-308.

Wiggins, G. & McTighe, J. (1998). *Understanding by design, (2nd Ed.).* Association for Supervision and Curriculum Development.

Wilcox, K., & Jeffery, J. (2014). Adolescents' writing in the content areas: National study results. *Research in the Teaching of English, 49*(2), 168-176.

Wilhelm, J. D. (2012). *Deepening comprehension with action strategies: Role plays, text-structure tableaux, talking statues, and other enactment techniques that engage students with text.* Scholastic Teaching Resources.

Wissinger, D. R., De La Paz, S., & Jackson, C. (2021). The effects of historical reading and writing strategy instruction with fourth-through sixth-grade students. *Journal of Educational Psychology, 113*(1), 49.

Zhang, J., & Dougherty Stahl, K. A. (2011). Collaborative reasoning: Language-rich discussions for English learners. *The Reading Teacher, 65*(4), 257-260.

Zhang, L. J., & Zhang, D. (2018). Metacognition in TESOL: Theory and practice. *The TESOL encyclopedia of English language teaching*, 1-8.

Zwiers, J. (2008). *Building academic language: Essential practices for content classrooms, grades 5-12.* Jossey-Bass.

BOOK ORDER FORM

Pricing, specifications, and availability subject to change without notice.

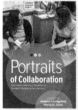
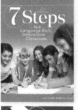
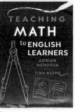

HOW TO ORDER

www.seidlitzeducation.com

CALL (210) 315-7119

FAX completed form to (949) 200-4384 with credit card info or attached purchase order

NAME

SHIPPING ADDRESS

CITY   STATE   ZIP

PHONE   EMAIL

Select payment method:

☐ Purchase Order attached
  please make P.O. out to Seidlitz Education

☐ Visa ☐ MasterCard ☐ Discover ☐ AMEX

CARD #

EXPIRES   CVV

SIGNATURE

TITLE	PRICE	QTY	TOTAL$
38 Great Academic Language Builders	$24.95		
7 Steps to a Language-Rich Interactive Classroom 2ND ED.	$32.95		
7 Steps To a Language-Rich, Interactive Foreign Language Classroom (LOTE)	$32.95		
Building Better Writers NEW!	$35.95		
Boosting Achievement: Reaching Students with Interrupted or Minimal Education	$26.95		
Content Review & Practice for the TX ESL 154 4TH ED.	$39.95		
Content Review & Practice for the TX Bilingual 164	$39.95		
Content Review & Practice for the TX Spanish 190	$39.95		
Diverse Learner Flip Book 2ND ED.	$29.95		
DIY PD: A Guide to Self-Directed Learning for Teachers of Multilingual Learners	$29.95		
ELLs in Texas: What Teachers Need to Know 2ND ED.	$34.95		
ELs in Texas: What School Leaders Need to Know 3RD ED.	$34.95		
ELPS Flip Book	$19.95		
English/Spanish Linguistic and Academic Connections	$29.95		
If You Only Knew: Letters from an Immigrant Teacher	$14.99		
Krofne with Baba NEW!	$18.95		
Juan José You Are Especial	$9.97		
Mi Cuaderno de Dictado SPANISH	$7.95		
Mi Cuaderno de Dictado KINDER SPANISH	$7.95		
Motivating ELLs: 27 Activities to Inspire & Engage Students	$26.95		
Navigating the ELPS: Using the Standards to Improve Instruction for English Learners	$24.95		
Navigating the ELPS: Math 2ND ED.	$29.95		
Navigating the ELPS: Science	$29.95		
Navigating the ELPS: Social Studies	$29.95		
Navigating the ELPS: Language Arts and Reading	$34.95		
Optimizando el desarrollo de la lectoescritura SPANISH	$39.95		
Pathways to Greatness for ELL Newcomers: A Comprehensive Guide for Schools & Teachers	$32.95		
Portraits of Collaboration	$32.95		
Reading & Writing with English Learners	$29.95		
RTI for ELLs Fold-Out	$16.95		
Sheltered Instruction in Texas: Second Language Acquisition Methods for Teachers of ELs	$29.95		
Small Moves, Big Gains: Teacher Habits that Help Kids To Talk More, Think More, Achieve More	$32.95		
Solved: A Teacher Guide to Making Word Problems Comprehensible	$26.95		
Talk Read Talk Write: A Practical Routine for Learning in All Content Areas K-12 2ND ED.	$32.95		
Teaching Math to English Learners	$24.95		
Teaching Social Studies to ELLs	$24.95		
Teaching Science to English Learners	$24.95		
¡Toma la Palabra! SPANISH	$32.95		
Visual Non-Glossary: Math 1 YR ONLINE LICENSE	$100.00		
Visual Non-Glossary: Science 1 YR ONLINE LICENSE	$100.00		
Visual Non-Glossary: Social Studies 1 YR ONLINE LICENSE	$100.00		
Visual Non-Glossary: All Content 1 YR ONLINE LICENSE	$250.00		
Vocabulary Now! 44 Strategies All Teachers Can Use	$29.95		
Workbook of Conversational Spanish for School Personnel LEVEL 1	$29.95		
Workbook of Conversational Spanish for School Personnel LEVEL 2	$29.95		

TAX EXEMPT? please fax a copy of your certificate along with order.	SUBTOTAL $
	DISCOUNT $
	SHIPPING $
SHIPPING 9% of order total, minimum $14.95 5-7 business days to ship. If needed sooner please call for rates.	TAX $
	TOTAL $

REV04/10/23

Pricing, specifications, and availability subject to change without notice.

TITLE	Price	QTY	TOTAL $
Instead Of I Don't Know Poster			
For the LOTE Classroom 24" x 36" | **3 pack**			
☐ LOTE FRENCH	$29.85		
☐ LOTE SPANISH	$29.85		
☐ LOTE GERMAN	$29.85		
☐ LOTE ARABIC NEW!	$29.85		
☐ LOTE CHINESE NEW!	$29.85		
	TOTAL		

TITLE	Price	QTY	TOTAL $
Instead Of I Don't Know Poster, 24" x 36" | **3 pack**			
☐ Elementary ENGLISH	$29.85		
☐ Secondary ENGLISH	$29.85		
Instead Of I Don't Know Posters, 11" x 17"| **20 pack**			
☐ Elementary ENGLISH	$40.00		
☐ Secondary ENGLISH	$40.00		
Instead Of I Don't Know Poster, 24" x 36" | **3 pack** Elementary SPANISH	$29.85		
Instead Of I Don't Know Posters, 11" x 17" | **20 pack** Elementary SPANISH	$40.00		
	TOTAL	**$**	

TITLE	Price	QTY	TOTAL $
Academic Language Cards and Activity Booklet, ENGLISH	$19.95		
Academic Language Cards, SPANISH	$9.95		
	TOTAL	**$**	

TITLE	Price	QTY	TOTAL $
Please Speak In Complete Sentences Poster 24" x 36" | **3 pack** ☐ ENGLISH ☐ SPANISH	$29.85		
Please Speak In Complete Sentences Posters,11" x 17" | **20 pack** ☐ ENGLISH ☐ SPANISH	$40.00		
	TOTAL	**$**	

TITLE	Price	QTY	TOTAL $
7 Steps to a Language-Rich, Interactive Classroom Poster 24" x 36" | **3 pack**	$23.85		
	TOTAL	**$**	

Developing language in every classroom.™

Seidlitz EDUCATION

HOW TO ORDER

www.seidlitzeducation.com

CALL (210) 315-7119

FAX completed form to (949) 200-4384 with credit card info or attached purchase order

TAX EXEMPT? please fax a copy of your certificate along with order.	GRAND TOTAL	$
	DISCOUNT	$
SHIPPING 9% of order total, minimum $14.95 5-7 business days to ship. If needed sooner please call for rates.	SHIPPING	$
	TAX	$
	FINAL TOTAL	$

NAME _____

SHIPPING ADDRESS _____

_____

CITY _____ STATE _____ ZIP _____

PHONE _____ EMAIL _____

Select payment method:

☐ **Purchase Order attached**
please make P.O. out to Seidlitz Education

☐ Visa ☐ MasterCard ☐ Discover ☐ AMEX

CARD # _____

EXPIRES _____ CVV _____

SIGNATURE _____